Roads Over Brown County

WINTER'S STORY

Also by T. C. Bartlett

SANDHILL PUBLISHERS

Young Adult
The Good Witch of the South

Children's Picture Books
It's Music Time
(Independent Publishers Book Awards Gold Medal Winner)

A Dog Named Zero and The Apple With No Name
(Voted by Kirkus Reviews as one of the Best Pictures Books of The Year)

You Can't Tickle Me
Never Was a Grump Grumpier
Eat, Eat, Eat! Cheese, Cheese, Cheese!
The Lost and Lonely Tumbleweed
Birds Fly A Cat Tries
The String
You Have to Do What I Say
Letting Go

THE CREATIVE COMPANY
& HARCOURT BRACE

Tuba Lessons
(Published in ten different languages)

For the love of the drive - TC

Roads
Over
Brown
County

Winter's Story

T. C. Bartlett

SANDHILL
PUBLISHERS, LLC
AN AMERICAN PUBLISHING COMPANY

First Edition - Hardcover
Book & Cover design by T. C. Bartlett
Cover & Interior Photos by Kim Gantt of Rokwon Images

Publishers website: sandhillpublishers.com
Sandhill Publishers, LLC, Nashville, Indiana

Editors: T. C. Bartlett, Kim Gantt & Holymell Edits

Printed in the United States of America
Library of Congress Preassigned Control Number: 2019942995
ISBN-13 978-0-9984716-1-7
ISBN-10 0-9984716-0-5

contents

PUBLISHER'S NOTE

The story you are about to read is one brief moment in the author's life. A story inspired by actual events in which the author recorded during his life of touring the country, working odd jobs and jotting down tales of the interesting people he encountered.

We have also included, sandwiched in between the chapters, excerpts from the author's travel journals.

Part One

Excerpt from the author's journal, Afterthoughts.

*We come and we go
I, like my mother and father before me
will become nothing more than the settling dust of the world . . .*

Excerpts from the author's journal, On The Road.

—Saturday
—High School Graduation Day (my birthday), May 13, 1972

Spent the day with my Martha.
Asked her if she would travel the world with me.
She couldn't. It hurt. But I understood.
Tomorrow, I knock the dirt of this sleepy little town off my shoes and
see what's out there.

* * *

—Saturday Night — My Birthday Present

Under the stars—shining, watching, listening—I gave my
virginity to my one true love, Martha.
And she gave me hers.
Blissfully we held each other (for how long I can't recall),
caught in the silence of the night,
clinging to the sparkling, tangled web of our love.

· · ·

— Mother's Day, Sunday, May 13, 1973

One year ago to this very day,
I made love under the stars with my darling Martha.
I had no idea then, it would be my only time.
I am lost without her (this is a dream), one day I will wake.

Prologue

Saturday, December 16
Early Morning; 7 AM — Sky leaden with winter overcast.
First words on paper.
Snow in the air. Much to write.
Excited and relieved to tell this tale . . .

My dear friend,

The morning opened gray. Clouds hung heavy, low and rippled, filled with the temper for longer, colder winter days and more snow to come. As I write this story for you, the ground is already covered in a thin blanket of white. The snowflakes floating down, one by one, are the fluffy kind, spinning slowly like miniature pinwheels, perching on branches and resting on the forest floor like soft, white, flaky dust.

"Ben left a note," she said as she handed me a cup of coffee and poured one for herself. "All he wrote was—" She hesitated, taking in a short breath and letting it out quickly. Then started over. "All Ben wrote was, 'I'm sorry'—nothin' more. Just, 'I'm sorry.'"

I'll never forget how her voice quavered when she told me

about the note. Or how her hands trembled, ever so slightly. Or how my body prickled. It cut me. God only knows the extent of her wound and the color of the blemish the note left behind.

I was standing by my studio window, elbows on the sash, resting my chin on laced fingers as if in prayer. The memory came from nowhere, like a slap. Even though time has moved forward (how many years is of no consequence), the image of that chilly October evening, when she told me about her past, is as bright in my mind as if the sun were shining, and I feel my face burn from the thought of it.

❧

As I scan the forest, a young doe, alone, makes her way through the woods, cautious, watchful. She stops—her ears prick. She stands still, head fixed forward, observing, questioning. She looks left then right. After a short pause, she lifts her nose and pulls in the wintery air, exhales, sending out a cloud of steam. She picks up her back leg and scratches her flank. She takes a cautious step forward, hesitates. Silence. She steps forward again. Stops. Her ears prick once more, and her tail stands at attention, showing the white underside, ready to run.

She looks left again, then right, searching. Perhaps a squirrel venturing out of its leafy nest to drink snow, or a possum scuttling off to its hovel, late for sleep. Her ears loosen, and her tail relaxes, twitching back and forth. Feeling safe for the moment, she drops her head to the ground and uses her nose to push away the blanket of white, down to the green hiding under the leaves for her morning breakfast.

It's not my intent to use the deer as a symbolic image or to imply it is an indirect suggestion of some cardinal meaning that forms a necessary base for the narrative I'm about to tell.

It's not.

I say: *Leave symbolism to the great authors who piss away their lives with alcohol, drugs, and torment, and let the ordinary, everyday scribbler like me (sober as the day I was born) write what we see and how we feel.* Sometimes, when an author places words on paper, the deer is just a deer, and the snow, well, the snow is just that—snow.

The beautiful scene that unfolded outside my window this morning was merely everyday life cautiously passing by at the exact moment I took a break from my writing, nothing more. It's not an uncommon occurrence to witness deer foraging in my backyard. Each and every time it happens, though, it makes me realize how fortunate I am to live in a home that presses lightly up against the fringe of a forest. And now you have that very same image in your mind of that one particular moment in my life, of that one particular deer roaming the woods behind my house.

I like knowing that. It makes me smile.

What intrigues me the most, though, when I am the recipient of such a tranquil winter scene, is I wonder what might be happening to everyone else in the world at that very moment I am a witness to such serenity. How many newborns opened their eyes to life and how many people closed them for their last.

&

I have a goal for this winter, which is to write this story before the birdsongs of spring. Even though every morning I rise early to begin my writing, as rigorously punctual as if I were punching a time clock, I fear this task may overwhelm me. I have stared at my journal on my writing desk and twirled my pencil in my hand for what seems like forever, tapping the eraser on the blank page like a drummer boy beating his snare marching into war, trying to decide how to place words in the right order to tell the tale of a woman chasing happiness.

✧

Happiness is a rare commodity indeed these days, especially in this fast-paced world of terrorism and skepticism, where personal commitment appears to be hurled over a cliff. True love seems only to happen in the movies, and raw passion only in romance novels.

At first, I had thought about calling this account of one woman's search for happiness a "love story." We have all had our own tribulations to contend with, had our hearts trampled on and broken because of love. We have all grown up thinking that one day we might even find our one true love. All of us have a love story to tell. And some of us enjoy reading a good love story. But I freely admit that love, especially romantic love, is devilishly difficult to write about.

This woman's tale, at least to me, is more than a love story. It isn't a tale of heroes and heroines or feats of great valor. It is a true story about one woman's pursuit of happiness along the roads of her life. From tragedy to triumph, from despair to hope, from heartbreak to love, where the events in her life gave birth to the person she is today.

As the world becomes more callous, this account about a sweet, sensitive, and charming countrywoman with pure, down-home country spirit—a meat and potatoes gal—almost made me believe in fairy tales.

Even though she lost her way for a time, she never gave up believing in the magic of possibility. She had moments that tested her character. But one day she did find her way back. She opened her arms and let love walk across her shadow and cast its spell, so all the tumblers could fall back into place and allow happiness to stay the heavy stones rattling inside her locked heart. It took great courage for her to do such a thing, to let love back in, and maybe, just maybe, capture her happily-ever-after.

Surprisingly, my friendship with this woman partly reshaped the way I view love, romance, and passion. Reducing my own personal disenchantment toward love just enough that I have recently been toying with the inclination to search for someone of the same mind who is compatible, congenial, and also hoping for the same sweet scent of affection. Someone who is willing to travel with me to the final moment, to hold my hand as I take my last breath, or I hers, as we drift off to heaven.

❧

Writing my reflections down on paper is not a natural process for me, especially when so many ideas fight against each other to be the first out.

I must warn you, I have a tendency to mix metaphors which might, for the most part, seem awkward at times. I am not a profound observer of life, and some of you I am sure will say my thinking and writing is conventional and rigid and that I often stumble over the edge of being cliché and fill my passages with banalities. But I love words and love stringing them together. Perhaps that, and the very facility I have with the written word are aspects you might find distracting. I hope not, and I do hope you'll forgive me for this and allow me some leeway in this regard. This story is but one short span in my life—a trickle if you will—written in the only way I know how to write. I can offer nothing more in my defense.

Every single English teacher I had in junior high and each in high school—especially those in high school—shook their fingers at me and scolded me time after time for my run-on sentences. I'd tell them: *Shake your finger as much as you like. I can't help myself.*

When I write, I am caught in the flow of the words, and I lose who I am and become fused, like two nuclei moving as one with the story—traveling through space and time—splashing through the edges of the universe, to sail beyond, like one ripple on a cosmic pond gently flowing outward in all directions forever and ever and ever . . .

My wordiness, well, think of it this way: I write my stories with a pencil. It is as if the graphite is an extension of my thoughts, and once the words are composed on paper, I have always believed they read the way I speak. One might argue it's my style, but I say it's merely me telling you one of my stories as if you were here sitting next to me.

XXIV

I am trying desperately not to rush, but I am flushed with worry and profoundly troubled that I will not be able to tell this tale in the way it has been so graciously related to me. As of late, writing my stories has become a daunting task. I do not feel at ease to explain the anxiety nipping at my heels, except to say: I feel like there's not much time left, it's late at night, and I am cramming for my final exam.

Despite my own personal insecurities, and what I'm about to face in my life, I sit here at my writing desk, looking out at the falling snow. A sweet emotion ripples through me about how this story has touched me, and how it has inspired me to give a kind reminder of my love to those I love so much.

When the time comes, I hope you, too, will be inspired and willing to give someone you genuinely care about a kind reminder of your love. A simple hug perhaps. Maybe a soft kiss on the cheek or a tender I-love-you whispered in the ear.

⁂

First things first, though—I have a need to tell you about the person I am.

Everyone starts out with dreams of what they hope their lives might become. I must confess, I never thought my life would end up the way it has. I've had a lot of high aspirations since my feet were firmly planted on the ground. I have been a figure skater, a figure skating coach, an abstract artist, a photographer, a mime, and once, tried acting. Believe it or not, I even earned my SAG card.

And during the years when I drifted from one town to the next, I have played many different roles. I've been a carpenter, a construction worker, a sanitation professional, a stock boy for department stores and grocery stores, a gas station attendant, a custodian (as I like to say, a custodial specialist), kitchen help on a cruise ship to Hawaii, and a landscaper. What the job was didn't matter to me: cleaning windows, scrubbing floors,vacuuming carpets, washing cars. I didn't care.

If I was paid to do it, I would do it the best I could, as long as it got me from one town to the next. I loved living on the road as an everyday handyman. But with all I have done in my life, there has been one passion that has walked shoulder to shoulder with me and has followed me everywhere, like a faithful companion—my love for writing. I am never without my journals or a pencil in my hand. The week after I received my high school diploma, I took off to follow all my passions, no matter where they would lead me.

Back then, I had such an eagerness to meet people and write their stories, no matter what their station in life might be—from hobo to commander in chief—they all had a story to tell.

❧

Some say I wear the soles of a gypsy, but gypsies find it challenging to make friends, for to do so gives too much of oneself away. Gypsies keep their secrets fiercely hidden, staying close to their own kind, roaming in packs, whereas a drifter is a solitary creature not afraid of making sincere, meaningful friendships.

So, yes, I am a drifter. Keeping a list of friends and addresses from across the country, in case one day, perhaps, I feel the need to revisit their doorsteps for another round of storytelling.

For years I drifted from one small town to another, picking up odd jobs here and there, and on occasion, performing pantomime in elementary schools. As long as you aren't picky, there is always a job to be found. Elementary schools didn't pay much for a mime performance, but any cold hard cash that put food in my mouth and gas in my truck worked for me.

The other advantage of being a drifter—at least for me—were the road trips, which produced an avid state of euphoria and satisfaction. Long drives settle my mind, altering the shape of my universe, giving me a chance to play with my dreams over and over. It has been one of the small pleasures in my life, land cruising in my faded rusty-red '54 half-ton pickup. I don't care what you might think about a truck.

A classic truck is timeless. It's sexy.

It's easy to work on.

Plus, I just looked good driving it.

I can't find the words to express the awakened spirit that flamed my soul when the rubber hit the road, and I trundled into a new town.

Even now, each time I get in my truck and switch it on, it's throaty growl speaks to me, persuading me, *Be bold, man!* And I can't help but feel that old sensation for a sweet, tender moment, that in-built hunger to take off and feel the magic of the drive. Yes, I still have my truck. I love my truck—the rumble of the engine makes me feel less alone, like the purr of a cat, or the hot water of a shower, or the heat from another body pressed firmly against mine in the dead of night.

My truck will be here long after I depart from this world. I restored it some years ago. It's no longer a rusty-red. Now, it looks better than I do, and runs better, too.

✌

Sittin' behind the wheel and drivin' until dawn or dusk tracks me down on a road I've never driven before, well, there's nothin' like it. (The hair on the back of my neck bristles and my shoulders shiver from the thought of it.)

It's not about the speed or the rush of the wind.

It's about takin' it easy, checkin' it all out.

It's about mobbin' the road—feelin' real—crusin' and bein' in control.

There's nothin' like exploring my country. Nothin' like watchin' the land roll by and seein' the snake-like pavement stretched out for miles ahead of me. Makes me feel a part of it, smack-dab in the middle of it, sloshin' and rollin' in the biscuits and gravy of it, sticky and gooey.

✌

There is an immeasurable charm betrothed to America, and it gives air to my lungs. Something so formidable no author can scratch pen across paper to describe its surprising diversity and overwhelming beauty—the complete opposite to my austere lifestyle and appearance. Seeing this vast and expansive land on the open road is, for lack of a better word, inspirational.

My days on the road filled me with wonder and delight. I genuinely got the feeling I was part of something great—something entirely and absolutely uniquely American. Each and every time I inhaled a capacious breath of America, I'd see a wistful misty fog rolling over a hillside, mysterious in its approach,

XXVIII

or another radiant western sky streaked with impossible shades of pinks and reds, inviting me to stop, take a private moment, reflect, and be awestruck all over again. And yet, there were times during those deep runs I'd say to myself, *"It'd be nice to have someone to share all this with and sit by my side. A woman by my side would be very nice. Very nice, indeed."* There is a sweeter taste of life when sharing it with someone you love.

All my life, I have been looking for that one place I could call my home and that one woman I could call my best friend. For a long time, no place knocked on my heart, except for two small towns and one city, Nashville, Indiana, Nantucket and Honolulu, Hawaii. Oh, the stories I could rattle off about Nantucket. Temptation played with my mind and tried to convince me to stay and start a life on Nantucket, but I didn't. Fodder for another time, perhaps. (Beware, that island is a bewitching siren and has the most seductive lure.) Needless to say, an unknown force pulled me away from Nantucket, threw me to the wolves in Hawaii, and then parked my keister in this small town of Nashville, here in Brown County, Indiana.

〜

The longing of mine to take to the road and move on, that itch to see what might be waiting for me at the next town is continually scratching at the edge of my thoughts, always nudging me to pack up and jump into my truck and hit the asphalt.

It is a difficult habit to break. There is a powerful voice ricocheting inside my head squeezing me, twisting my feelings and wrapping itself tightly around my ear, like a cold hard nagging whisper. *"Move on."* it says to me, *"Move on."* This time, however, I decided to ignore it. But I was torn, because moving from town to town had become a part of me, no different than a limb attached to my body. There was no denying it, though, I'd been seduced by this little town of Nashville that rests peacefully along old State Road 135, hidden in a small wooded valley—an old-time artist colony. Blink, and you'd miss it. Large sycamore and maple trees stand tall along its main street, a short, not even half-mile-long thoroughfare. It has one intersection which cuts the town right in half with its one traffic light, and its Brown County stone buildings and log cabin stores neatly line up in rows, made for tourists to spend their money.

When I rolled into Nashville, I had been traveling around the country searching for that one place for what seemed like an eternity. It was Autumn. The air clean and fresh. The entire town dipped in colors, trees on fire. I was instantly taken. It was as if the town placed its soothing hand into mine and brushed the road dust off my shoulders. There was something about this place, something about this Brown County, the town of Nashville, something about the music of the countryside sang to me. So, I chose to sing along and decided to stay a while and find out whether I believed one place could cool the drifting spirit that dogged me and tugged at the cuff of my pants.

I liked the people in this town. I liked their easy country manner and was touched by their small-town hospitality that had grown on me quickly, like sweet corn in the summer.

≪⑤

In this progressively insensitive and sometimes vicious world,

XXX

we often hide behind our hard outer shells and tough-skinned sensibilities. We don't readily open our doors wide enough to let love flow through because we fear our secrets, things we long for will be taken advantage of, torn apart, and scattered to the wind.

In spite of our fears, we continually hope, dream, and wish for that one Prince Charming, or that one Cinderella, to kiss our lips and repair our broken wings. I'm talking about the stuff fairy tales are made of—at some point in our lives, don't we all dream of such fairy sightings? I suppose some do, and some don't. I prefer to believe in the fairy-tale ending, and not duckwalk in shallow dreams.

For me . . . well, I am such a softy I can get that same heartfelt ache when I watch *America's Got Talent* and a thirteen-year-old girl plays an electric ukulele, sings a song she wrote herself, and one judge pushes the golden buzzer. The audience roars with excitement for her, and my eyes leak. Yes, I am a pushover when it comes to things of the heart.

❦

The snow is coming down much harder now, so many flakes that when I look out my window, I feel like I'm looking through lace curtains. I love this time of year. But what I most sincerely wish in the writing of this tale of woe and perseverance, and with a little luck thrown my way—if there is such a thing—is that you find pleasure in the reading.

One last thought—at least, for now . . .

Many stories glide free of charge along the country roads that gently meander all through this part of southern Indiana.

With each breath you drink in, you can taste the magic that lives and breathes in the hills and hollers♦ here in Brown County. All anyone has to do is let themselves be touched by that drifting magic to know it's true. I believe you will see that stories like this one travel untethered throughout time, give us hope, and make us admit—perhaps, one day—good things can happen to us all.

♦ hollers: The vernacular used in southern Indiana for "hollow": a small valley or ravine.

It is the unexpected
that adds mystery to our lives
It is hope
that makes life tolerable
It is love
that makes life sing . . .

Excerpts from the author's journal, Skaters Rule.

—Saturday, May 20, 1972

Drove down to Kentucky to meet my skating partner for practice today. Instead of practicing, I dumped her. Should have been smart enough to have done so years ago.

Tired of her highbrow, southern-gal, tiara-wearin', queen-like attitude and treating me like her slave. Whatta spoiled bitch.

Frittered away a lot of time.

Need to move on . . .

* * *

—Friday, June 02, 1972

Just arrived in Squaw Valley for their skating summer school. I still have some competitive spirit left in me. Maybe do dances and pairs this time.

Why the hell not.

Besides, I love being in the mountains.

The fresh air. Clean. With the scent of pine.

Calms me down. A man could find peace here.

—Thursday, August 03, 1972

I've been invited to train with Mr. Don Beared in Wilmington, Delaware, at his skating facility. His students call him Bear. He is one of the top coaches in the world. A real ladies' man. A lot of political pull. A Powerful presence. This coach makes champions.
He wants me to be at his rink before the end of the summer so I can try-out with a couple of skating partners, he thought would be a good match.
I plan on going and seeing where it takes me.
I wish my Martha could be here with me in Squaw Valley to see all the high-level skaters. It's really a rush.
I called her last night and asked once more if she'd travel the rest of her life with me. She said no again. Still hurts.
Need to relax. Keep cool. Keep focused.
Must find myself and figure out who I am, where I'm going, and skate my everlovin' buns off.

———————

Excerpt from the author's journal, On The Road.

— Saturday, October 13, 1973

Returned home for my dear Martha's funeral . . .
Killed in a car accident . . .
Drunk driver . . .
One second she was alive, and in the next, she was gone forever.
There will never be another like her to make love to my mind, hold my heart in her thoughts, and show me how to live.

CHAPTER 1

Winter

Tuesday, January 09
After Lunch: Ready to write.
Had my favorite, grilled cheese sandwich with bacon and tomato
on whole wheat. Pigged out and made two! More snow on the
way. Maybe another eight inches . . . perfect . . .

The woman in this story reminds me of the seasons. She is like the summer, with heat and strength; she is the fall, showing all the colors of her personality; like the spring, fresh and unpredictable. Mostly, though, she reminds me of winter, forlorn and haunted by misfortune.

She is a fiercely private woman, which I will respect by not revealing her given name, and also because I know the effort it takes for someone to confide in me about what they've endured chasing after happiness.

It is not easy for any person to open their heart when it has been so trampled upon.

I will call her Winter . . .

. . . not because sorrow had spilled into her life, but because winter is one of my favorite seasons. Something about winter

37

days touches me so. The beauty after an ice storm when the trees weep with ice, or when the snow blankets everything, muffling out all the world's problems—the stillness, the silence, protected—it is a hush that cuffs playfully inside me, makes me pause, smile, and fills me with hope.

The one time I didn't like snow was when I was a kid. And that's because back then Indiana schools were hardly ever canceled when it snowed.

Every kid wanted to stay home from school when that white flaky stuff floated around in the air and covered the ground. There wasn't such a thing as a snow emergency, and we didn't have a clue what a wind chill factor was. We went outside and froze our asses off.

Mothers all across Indiana would bundle kids up, put a scarf around their necks, and shove them out the door into the Arctic-like freeze and say, "It's not that cold—now go on, don't dawdle, you get!"

We'd grit our chattering teeth, leaning into the wind, and we'd dawdle, but not for long. With eyes stinging in the frigid temperature, icicles forming on our eyelashes, we cussed all the while under our frozen breath wishing we could stay home and have a snowball fight with our buddies. But with each heavy footfall, we realized we had no choice but to trudge our way through the drifts of white and get our frozen butts to school.

Sorry, I digress. Back to Winter . . .

🙠

When I first set eyes on Winter, she looked as if a gust of wind could blow her away. She was a sweet, tiny thing, maybe five feet, if that. I asked her once how short she was—*short* might not have been the best choice of words. "You must be, what . . . four foot somethin'?" She looked at me like I didn't have a clue how to talk to a woman, especially a country girl. She pulled out her driver's license, held it out to me, blood flaming in her cheeks and said, "Go on. Take it! That's right. Five feet—not four foot somethin'!" Her sexy lips creased into a sly, *now whatta y'all gotta say for yourself, you dumb hick* smile.

The sense I had that she might be a lightweight got shot to hell when she pulled that driver's license out like a sheriff's badge and rubbed that smirk of hers into my face. She made it clear it would take a Dorothy Gale–sized cyclone to push her over.

What made me laugh at myself was that I towered over her five foot nothin' frame with all my wiry six feet (as long as I didn't slouch I made six feet, that is), at least that's what *my* driver's license says, six feet zero inches, brown hair and blue eyes. No in between—like pale blue or light blue, or startling, sexy blue—just blue. I smiled back, accepting defeat to keep the peace. I loved her spunkiness, but in my mind, Winter had to be shorter than five feet. I'm sure someone who issued her the license added the half inch for her. Probably a love-struck nerd who had a wasteful wish she might go out with him one day. I wouldn't blame the guy for a second.

I would've done the very same thing.

❧

Winter had haunting green eyes that glowed as if sunshine

shone behind them, and her hair was that of a fiery red sunset that shimmered as if it might at any moment crackle and burst into flame, a bewitching comparison to her smooth, pale skin, the pallor of someone who rarely spent time outdoors. Which was far from the truth since she was born and raised on a farm.

Her long hair purposely rolled over her shoulders and half-way down her back, with a straight cut so precise not one single strand appeared longer than the other. Small, faded freckles dotted the bridge of her nose and grazed the top of her cheeks. Her soft mouth was made for seductive smiles, and she had one dimple that sparkled when she laughed, a laugh so tempting that men were quickly drawn in by the intense impulse to hold her in their arms. But it was the color of her eyes and hair that stood out. Her large sizzling, green eyes and striking red hair forced everyone she'd meet to do at least one double take.

I could tell, without a doubt, Winter knew how to defend herself, and when it was warranted, she could be a fearsome, bristly tempest of a woman. For such a petite thing, she'd knock your eyes to the back of your skull if she thought you deserved it. That strength could have been the country girl part of her, or perhaps, something born from what life had placed in front of her. Whatever it may have been, Winter was unlike any other woman I had met in my life. She pulled me into her.

Deep in.

Without even trying.

꿍

During my travels I have met people, like Winter, who are plain speaking and honest to a fault. Then something awful happens that makes them lose faith in themselves, or in God, or the hope of ever meeting a perfect someone.

Even though Winter is the focus of my story, I want to describe a few of my coworkers and where I had been working at the time when I met Winter. I'd gotten a job as one of the set-up guys at the Abe Martin Lodge, in Brown County.

My duties were pretty straightforward. I set up tables and chairs for meetings, weddings, and anything in between. I also became one of the part-time maintenance men—once a handyman, always a handyman. Brown County has a state park which consists of more than 17,000 acres of a lush hardwood forest that borders the town limits of Nashville. Nestled in one corner of that forest is the lodge.

I had been working at the lodge for the better part of two years. It had been the longest I had ever been in one place, except for Nantucket, since I'd left my childhood home in the summer of '72.

∽

Writing about those I shared my work day with doesn't necessarily add depth to my tale in any particular way, except to say that it might help kindle a particular flavor.

They were good, simple folks, hard-working, doing the best that they could for their families and themselves. They brought color to my life and telling you a little about them keeps their spirit alive. I learned to admire and respect some of my workmates, while others I learned to keep at a distance. We were a small group of misfits, but not Winter, she was something more, uncommon, especially for a farm girl slinging hash at the lodge.

&

It was a late morning work break. A couple of days after the Fourth of July. A few of us, including Winter, were sitting out on the loading dock sucking in the humid midsummer air and talking about how we were still finding beer cans hidden all around the lodge after the independence day celebration.

Summer's hot breath can sit so heavily and thick with moisture among the trees in this part of the forest; you can cut it with a knife and squeeze it like a sponge. But on that day, thank goodness, the humidity wasn't so bad as long as you didn't move around that much.

I don't smoke, but the others around me did, and since the loading dock had been the one place we were officially allowed to take our breaks, those who didn't smoke would hang out with those who did, and we all got along. All that mattered was having a moment to clear our minds or (for the smokers) to get a nicotine fix to carry on for the rest of the day.

Winter, off to my right, sat on the only chair, a rickety, lopsided discard from the recreation room, no longer decent enough for the guests of the lodge. She was teetering on the back two legs with one arm stretched out on the railing for counterbalance taking slow vigilant puffs from her cigarette, watching everyone with a judicious squint. After each observant puff, wispy smoke swirled and clouded around her and vanished, swallowed by the moisture-filled air. I could see her green eyes through the smoky haze, sparkling like jewels from the sun.

That green.

Her eyes.

They tormented me. But only I could hear the thumping and feel the clatter of my heart when she'd cast that green my way.

Simon, the other set-up guy, stood to my left, one elbow supporting his weight on the railing that separated our outdoor break space from the grease bins. With closed eyes, he slowly slid a coffin nail across his upper lip, taking in the aroma of the nicotine-bathed tobacco before lighting up. Opposite Simon and me, a gaggle of housemaids chatted and puffed while sitting on a makeshift bench made out of a ten-foot-long plank of treated pine laid slapdashed on cinder blocks.

Simon was country-born through and through, and he never placed a worry on his shoulder when asked to do a favor. Someone you could rely on entirely, without hesitation. He was a downright, honest-to-goodness, gettin' by, good-ole country boy. A stout, thick-boned man, hovering somewhere between forty and fifty years of age, clean-shaven, eyes continuously bloodshot around the edges, but gentle in their gaze.

A heavy drinker? Yes.

But never tipsy at work.

A heavy smoker? Without a doubt.

The years of cigarettes and beer had been slowly adding weight to his frame, adding inches to his hardpan beer belly, and patches of wrinkles to his face.

I felt Simon saw life during the day through a haze from an evening of beers, and he regularly flirted with the ladies like it was a badge of honor. The girls at the lodge took it in stride, never offended by Simon's philandering. Actually, a few looked forward to it and reciprocated with some good-ole country girl flirting of their own.

∾

Most of the women who worked as housemaids were plump and round, like sweet-vine tomatoes, rolling through the lodge, skillfully cleaning guest bedrooms day in and day out with little or no complaint.

But one in particular, Natty—curvy and buxom—was more the shape of a lemon, and sour to the taste. Bitching and chirping about everything, and always pissed off. Natty didn't roll. She shifted from side to side. When she spoke, the puffed out jello-like fold under her chin would jiggle like the fleshy wattle hanging from the neck of a chicken.

What bothered me the most about Natty was that she relentlessly borrowed money for her lunch, and Simon was her primary target. Bummed cigarettes, too. When I first started at the lodge, Natty asked me for money, and I flat out said, "I don't give out loans to moochers." Okay, I didn't call her a moocher, but I thought it. Then she asked to bum a cigarette, "Don't smoke," I told her. "Never have." Needless to say, after that encounter we rarely spoke.

I didn't like her.

Doubted if I ever would.

Untrustworthy.

Usually, I'm pretty easy-going; staying in the background and keeping an open mind about people. But Natty, she could rub a person's patience raw, right down to the nub. Like a chigger bite: itchy, incredibly annoying, something you try to ignore, but can't, until you scratch it so much it welts and bleeds the life out of you.

She knew Simon was a soft touch and that he'd always oblige her. She would toy with him just enough to make him think he'd be getting a lot more in return for giving her the loose change jingling around in his pocket. I hated watching Natty take advantage of Simon like that. I asked him once, "Why do you let Natty do you like that?"

He replied, "Natty has less than me."

The thing was, Simon had less to give than anyone, except for his kindness. He lived in a small, run-down, rusty trailer. Barely big enough for one person. A grayish-green mold clung to its sides, which grew more each day. It had a blue plastic tarp that covered holes in the roof and a plywood door to keep the winter wind from howling in. And he had a beat-up truck (rust eating away the wheel wells), that was either broken down most of the time or loaned out to a friend.

I don't have enough fingers and toes to count how many times I picked Simon up for work because a friend, or a friend of a friend, needed to use his truck. I suppose it was indicative of Simon's character that he helped people with a measure of decency, even though they took more from him than he received.

So there we were. Not all, but some of us. Taking a break from the drudgery of the day, soaking in the hot soggy air and inhaling tobacco smoke. We were the bone and marrow of the Abe Martin Lodge that kept the blood running through its veins. A sorry lot for sure, but a group that got the job done well enough. All in all, I liked my coworkers. Never spent time with them away from the lodge, except of course, every now and then to give Simon a ride to work, or a ride home.

The unmistakable cawing of Natty clamored through the loading dock doors as she shouted over her shoulder at one of the cooks who stood slack-jawed in the kitchen hallway, vigorously protesting that it wasn't her fault. The door shut before she'd finished her sentence leaving the cook nothing more to do but to fume back into the kitchen.

As I watched Natty make her thunderous entrance, my face scrunched and I thought . . . let's just say it wasn't a pleasant thought. Not worth repeating.

I raked my hands through my hair and felt it bristle. It was full and starting to get out of control. I needed to get it cut. I like going to a local barbershop for a cut and a shave. Small town barbers remind me of country preachers. They shave your sins away with hot lather and a straight razor. Makes me feel civilized to have a barber give me a shave once in a while. Smooth. Clean. Ready for a soft cheek from a pretty girl. I decided to do that the next morning before work.

A nearby bird fluttered and I turned toward the noise, curious about the ruckus. An irate house sparrow flapped out from under the corner of the rain gutter where it had been perched, eyeing everyone.

Waiting.

Watching.

It dive-bombed to the ground, chasing another sparrow

from a breadcrumb. Such fluttering skirmishes happened all the time on the dock since trash bags were hastily dragged across it, heedlessly bounced down the stairs before being thrown away, leaving bits of discarded food in their wake.

Out of the corner of my eye, I followed Natty as she minced her way to an opening on the flimsy, jury-rigged bench. She wiggled her copious mass to make more room for herself and plopped down. The two-by-twelve sagged and groaned and trembled on the cinder block legs, threatening to shatter, jiggling the doughy folds of the other ladies sitting on the bench.

Every time Natty crept her way into my skull, I wondered how many work uniforms she must have ruined where her rippling waves of skin and pockets of flesh had popped buttons and split seams.

❧

Natty's crow-like eyes, black, and piercing, raked over Simon. Simon shot back a weak smile, anticipating what Natty was about to ask. Natty's lips moved and released the same question she'd ask Simon every time she'd brush past him, "Can I bum a smoke?" Simon shooed a fly from his ear, broke away from the railing, and gave Natty a cigarette.

"Thanks, hun," she cooed. "You're so good to me. Always gotta smoke ready—sweet thing." She winked and patted herself down like she was looking for some matches.

Part of me wanted to whack Natty upside the head and whittle her bulk down a couple of sizes.

I didn't.

Wouldn't.

I'd never hit a woman.

Never have, never will. But Natty, well, Natty was one woman I wanted to shake hard to force some manners into. She was a youngster, maybe twenty-three (looked like forty with the extra weight and butter belly on her), but being young didn't give Natty an excuse for her tawdry behavior.

Simon handed Natty his Bic lighter and stepped back to his perch while she fired up her gasper. She took a strong toke, and added, while smoke escaped as she talked, "I wuz in such a rush this mornin', bein' late 'n' all, I left them damn smokes on the counter. Musta left them damn matches there, too." Natty took in a long healthy drag. The ash end of the Marlboro turned a bright red and sizzled. After she filled her lungs, she blew smoke out the side of her mouth, raised her eyebrows, put Simon's Bic in her pocket, winked, and turned to talk to one of the girls, forgetting about Simon the second she'd inhaled.

I thought, hell, if Simon had the ability to understand and show such compassion toward Natty, maybe I could.

I tried, but it didn't take.

As the weeks passed, I liked her less and less. Funny how the mind can go venomous so quickly with some people, while others comfortably stick to your spirit like Velcro.

❧

Then there was Ash. Ash was one of the dishwashers for the lodge—a big, burly, middle-aged man with a baleful face, restless and dangerous eyes, curly black hair, and eyebrows that reached across his forehead.

Yes, he was a unibrow dude, shy and soft-spoken.

I liked him.

Even though I never had a conversation with him, I could tell the minute we met he had a kind soul. When you greeted Ash with "Good-mornin'," he'd nod his head thinly, eyes firmly fixed on the ground, and go about his business. But you would know his nod was sincere.

He stood off to the far side of the loading dock, away from all the others, head tilted down, gaze swimming among the cracks in the concrete and spilled grease. He had one leg bent with his foot resting on the wall and was forcefully taking one last draw from his Marlboro (the choice cancer stick of the lodge), filling his lungs with smoke, filling them full, then holding it—holding it—and letting it out in one long burst, as if it were the last puff of his life. When he'd emptied his lungs, he turned his head just a tad—no one noticed except me—stealing a disapproving glance at Natty.

Another reason why I liked him.

He reminded me of a mangy stray, alone, frightened, feral to a point—aloof most the time—beaten down by life. His food-splattered wash-apron covered most of his round beer belly, except for what oozed out from the sides. His belt never did justice to his oversized wrinkled work trousers that sagged way below his tailbone, liquefying into folds like the face of an old bloodhound.

Everything about Ash seemed to be melting away—rounded shoulders, head always posed downward like he was hoping to find some precious jewel or a few lost coins. He wore a long-sleeved red and black checkered cotton shirt—sleeves rolled up to his elbows—that had been washed so many times its plaid design had turned a faded pink and gray. His shirttail hung loose, abandoned, and a couple seams were splitting apart, frayed into neglected tufts. And his hands weathered, cracked, leathery from drowning in the sludge of dirty dishes and scalding water.

Ash walked past me, reached down to the ashtray, and pushed his cigarette butt into the humidity-soaked sand with his thumb, grinding it back and forth to put it out. I watched it smolder, smoke floating like a ghostly figure around his hand and wondered how many packs a day he might smoke, and how much that must cost him—it probably took a third of his pay from throwing suds on dishes all day and countless late evenings.

I don't have a clue what it's like to feel nicotine whip me into obedience. I am sure Ash felt buying as many packs as he needed to feed his habit was money well spent. One day he might quit. If the world would just rest for a while—just be still for a matter of months, maybe he could. We all make our choices in life, and that was his. At any rate, who am I to question anyone who smokes?

Ash walked through the door and disappeared back to his suds and hot water. Winter watched him with interest, too, and mentioned how Ash reminded her of Lennie. She didn't say anything else, just, "That guy reminds me of Lennie."

I knew right away she was comparing Ash to the character from the book *Of Mice and Men*. And she was right about the big, burly dishwasher. He did remind me of Lennie. An older, hammered-down and hard-ridden Lennie.

In that one statement, I knew Winter was a woman of

depth. A lot more refined than she let on. She kept her intel-
ligence locked away, protected, and, maybe without meaning to
do so, now and then her smarts would sneak out and spill on
the ground for someone like me to scoop up.

Part of me thinks she said it to see if I got the reference she
made to *Of Mice and Men.* You know, to put measurement to
me—size me up, as it were. Who knows? It was an odd little
quirk in her personality I caught wind of. It wasn't a bad thing.
Interesting, that's all. Something I think not many people
noticed about her.

But I did.

Before she said it, she lifted her cigarette to her mouth taking her time about inhaling and tossed a quick gander in my
direction. But I pretended I hadn't noticed her glance. Maybe
she was testing me, I don't know. Smart people are like that
sometimes, poking around about their favorite topics or hob-
bies, or quoting a famous person, or throwing out a phrase
from Shakespeare, just a light tap—to see if people are up for
the challenge.

When no one agreed with her observation of the dishwasher, she shook her head and let the moment drift away, as effortlessly as she did when she put her cigarette out and walked back
inside the lodge to continue her day.

Generally, I find a woman's attractiveness tempered by a
cigarette stuck between sensual lips. Smoking is not something
I ever found appealing, but with Winter I let it slide. There was
so much more going on for her that a bad habit didn't seem
to matter all that much to me. There are always exceptions to
the rules we make for ourselves—some rules are meant to be

broken. I looked at her cigarette butt—no lipstick.

I liked that.

I liked that a lot.

I had a feeling I could break a lot of rules when it came to Winter.

✍

Guys like me always like to think charm and persistence will make any girl turn our way. For me, nearly any beautiful woman could make me stay longer in one place than I had initially planned. I had been thinking for a long time how nice it would be to have someone special to share my life with. Someone who could look me in the eye and see me for the man I indeed was, or the man I could become.

I believe Winter was that kind of woman. The thing about Winter was that she could make a man react on impulse rather than using the ability to respond rationally. She could knock common sense right out of a man quickly—very quickly. She could make a man stutter, lose his train of thought, and make him act like an idiot before he knew what had happened to him. She could look a man square in the eye and size 'em up or cut 'em down a couple of notches.

She was also the type of woman a man could effortlessly fall for and find love with, and part of me was under the delusion that I might have a shot with her.

Strange isn't it, how some people bring out the light while others—like Natty—lurk around corners and walk in shadow?

Winter brought out the light in a man.

She brought the light out in me.

She rattled my bones. Twisted my toes.

Every time we spent time together, Winter jumbled my emotions—butterflies everywhere. Each time I laced her into my thoughts, my mind would flutter and swell like a gutter after a rainstorm. She captured my heart with a great *whoosh*. There was no doubt in my mind whatsoever;

I was falling into Winter, hard and fast.

❧

Speaking of acting like an idiot, the following week, I gave Winter a copy of *Of Mice and Men*.

I even put a cloth ribbon around it, with a sweet note attached. A pink ribbon, if you were wondering.

I made it all girly-like. Stop laughing.

At the time, I thought it was a good idea. But she didn't react much to the gift: "Thanks," is all she said, and went back to work, leaving me off balance. Like I said, Winter had a way of making a man feel like an idiot.

Not the best way to start a friendship.

Easy enough to recover from, though.

My biggest problem has always been that I have a tendency to fall for certain women about as hard as I fall for certain books. Books for me have such a robust and seductive tug of mystery. I had hoped Winter had the same problem with men as I have with women and the same seductive attraction to books.

I am pretty sure she did.

Books, I thought, would be something we could share as

friends with the wishful hope of something more. When first getting to know Winter and based on my gift-giving blunder, I was equally confident, there was no way in hell she'd divulge her secrets to me.

At least not yet. I still had hope and willing to wait.

Yeah, I know what you're thinking. The book with the ribbon was a sorry ass move on my part. Sometimes a man has to wear a woman down, inch-by-inch, with our natural charm and lame moves. Alas, nothing I tried worked on Winter.

The reality that Winter and I were going to be kindhearted friends and not lovers slapped me in the face faster than cold water from a country creek.

And that was fine. Well, fine enough.

I could learn to live with it.

&

I often wondered if Winter knew she had power over me.

Most women do, I think.

I am pretty sure she could feel the heat from my eyes when I'd steal a glance her way like a gobsmacked, star-struck fan when she took a customer's order, cleaned tables, or swept the floor. I know sex in and of itself isn't love, but in a pinch it'll do, and in my case, love was—is—something I have always dreamed of, wished for, and chased after. And with Winter it wasn't about sex. It was deeper than that. Stronger than that.

Sometimes though, when men and women are becoming friends, there is a sexual spark present. Nothing romantic in nature, just an electrical charge that acknowledges the attraction. If that spark ignites, the friendship can gallop from a com-

fortable connection and friendly hugs to naked in bed, engag-
ing in the most intimate of acts. But the daylight hours can
make a person realize they'd just lost a unique and special bond
with a unique and extraordinary friend.

Being amatory with Winter would have changed everything
that was becoming special between us. Typically, I would throw
caution to the wind and let the sparks fly with a beautiful woman. But not with Winter. I wasn't going to tempt fate and reck-
lessly fritter away the close bond I was beginning to feel for her.

She was fresh, minty air for me and I had no idea where my
wannabe relationship would take me, but as it was right then, I
honestly liked her—a lot—and wanted to spend as much time
as I possibly could with her, naked or otherwise.

I truly wanted us to be good-ole work buddies who liked
to take a break from our lives once in a while and take a moment to sit and talk. Or not talk at all, and enjoy the silence of
hanging with a good friend. That alone was something unusual
enough, unique enough that would bind us together and would
ground us, and was ours and ours alone. Something that let us
know there was so much more to our lives than the sometimes
painful numbing cruelty of passing the time working at a job
that only supplied us with a meager paycheck twice a month.

❧

It was my second encounter with Winter that makes me laugh
at myself from time to time.

I had been cleaning and moving tables non-stop from the
moment I arrived at work in the morning. Just before sunrise.
I was thirsty. I needed my sugar fix. My drink of choice, a nice

cold Pepsi. And any excuse I allowed myself, I seemed to end up in the kitchen where I knew I'd have the best chance to sneak an eyeful of Winter. Plus, I'm addicted to Pepsi, which I felt entitled me to frequent trips to the kitchen to ease my sugary habit and satisfy my sweet tooth. (My dependency for a Pepsi is no different than my desire for a pretty woman. They're both bad for me, but I can't help myself.)

The soda dispenser was located in a narrow nook sitting next to the coffee station, directly opposite the swinging kitchen doors. Shelves on the facing wall were packed with paper coffee cups, Styrofoam drink cups, and takeout boxes. The waitress Beth (who'd been slingin' hash right out of high school), was at the coffee station pouring coffee for her order.

She was a tall string bean of a gal (perfect for wigglin' in and out of the nook), and a smile that went from ear to ear that would convince you to get a pile of crispy critters along with the fried chicken. She was kind and understanding and made you feel like you'd just eaten in the best restaurant in the county.

She told me her age once, but I don't remember, thirty-something, I think. I do remember she had six kids—all girls—no husband, and a ton of energy like she didn't have an off switch and very proud of her Hoosier heritage. The fourth generation she told me once with a toothy grin that left lipstick on her ears. That I will never forget. I liked her. Respected her a lot, and when she brought her girls to the lodge for the dinner buffet, they followed her around like ducklings all in a row.

ૐ

The nook's small signature made it difficult for more than one person to navigate within its borders at the same time, really too narrow for two people unless you didn't mind rubbing against someone else.

When the restaurant was busy, it was like watching a tag-team wrestling match with the waitresses. And the thought of taking advantage of the nook's narrowness to get close and personal with Winter never entered my mind.

Okay, maybe it did—for a second.

All right, maybe two seconds.

But that's beside the point.

Beth skirted off with coffee in hand. I started to fill my drink cup when Winter reached in to do the same. Because of the nook's tight quarters, and because I am the gentleman that I am, I backed out of her way. When I gave her more space, she said in a mocking and somewhat determined-to-figure-me-out way, "Do I scare you?"

"Yeah, right," I said with a huff, trying to hide my discomfort while butterflies flopped around in my stomach. "A guy with a chainsaw wearing a hockey mask scares me." I smiled and added, "You—you only frighten me." A slight smile played around her lips, too.

Generally, when butterflies are all scattered about flying nervously inside me, I force them to fly in formation and stay cool and collected. Not so with Winter. That's because women I really, really like *do* frighten me. I always feel gawky around women who make my heart skip a beat or two. And Winter made me feel pretty damn gawky.

Here's the thing, I gave her more room in the nook so she wouldn't have to deal with some dude rubbing up against her.

That's the truth. Not that I would have minded a close encounter, or should I say: a little nookie in the nook—it was my way of showing the chivalrous side of my personality. Most women appreciate that in a man.

Not Winter.

As far as Winter was concerned, I looked like one big, nerdy Twinkie.

Thank goodness I had a witty reply.

Well, witty enough to make her smile and for me to keep a semblance of dignity. No man is *ever* enthusiastic about the possibility of looking like a Twinkie in front of a pretty woman.

But I think it was my lame move with the book gift and my good sense of humor that helped pave the way for her to accept me as a friend. Or maybe it was when I covered her car with over a hundred daffodils? Or the tailgate lunches we had using my truck in the middle of the parking lot at the lodge.

Funny thing was, once I gained her trust, asking her out on a real date didn't seem right. And, before we became "just friends," I wasn't embarrassed when she turned me down those times I did try . . . hold on . . . I take that back.

It did fluster me. A little. But I never let her know that.

✍

As the days rolled forward, so did our friendship—small steps for sure.

She forgave me straightaway for all the idiot moves I used on her, and we'd laughed about them over coffee. She never toyed with me or took advantage of the fact that she knew I could like her more than "just being friends," and she never made me feel beneath her.

I loved her smile when she laughed.

So real.

Candid.

Or when she'd bump my shoulder with hers for no reason. Needless to say, it took over six months for Winter to decide I was a decent enough guy to spend time with.

We grew to respect each other.

Every healthy friendship requires mutual respect.

The sad thing was, I thought we'd be a perfect match because we both preferred to be connoisseurs of a cold bottle of beer and a good read, rather than a couple of uptight, fermented grape oenophiles who liked smelly cheese.

She once asked, leaning in close to me. "Do your lame moves actually work on girls?"

"Normally," I responded, leaning closer. Then I added, "You're having coffee with me, aren't you?"

"That's 'cause I feel sorry for ya," she said, patting me on my hand and giving me a sly but friendly smile and a quick flirtatious wink. I laughed at myself for thinking how her simple spicy wink sent shivers through me.

When we sat down together for our visits, we were never distracted by our surroundings and we talked about simple things—the weather, the age of trees, the ins and outs of small-town life, the gossip rolling through the lodge and over the hills and hollers of Brown County.

As we got to know each other better, we talked about my travels across the country and how I loved writing stories about the people I met along the way.

"Maybe I could write Winter's story one day," I suggested once.

"Me?" She shook her head in a gentle, sensitive way. "No. I'm no one special." She was quiet for a second and then asked, "Why would you want to write about me, anyway?"

"A guy broke into Simon's home when he was fourteen years old. His older brother stabbed the guy in the back thirty-eight times. The judge ruled it wasn't self-defense. Simon's brother was eighteen and is doing life plus sixty, with no parole."

"I had no idea," she said.

"Everybody's got a story," I replied. Her lips turned down at the corners, ever so slightly, into a frown that caught me off guard. But there was a glimmer in her eyes that made me think—just for an instant—she might be willing to tell me her story.

So I asked. "What happened to you, Winter? "

Her eyes shifted and went flat, cryptic.

I could feel it. She was holding back.

Something she fought to keep in the dark.

Something painful. Something tragic.

From the very moment our eyes found each other, Winter always seemed like she was hiding something about her past. Truthfully, I sensed it before we had ever gotten to know each other. The way she carried herself. The way she didn't eye me straight on when she talked to me but seemed to be staring off in the distance, past me.

Was I prying because I wanted to know more about her?

Yes, and no. Plus, part of me was merely curious.

Did I think she was going to open up to me and tell me all

her secrets?

No, Not really.

Did I press her anymore on it?

Absolutely not.

Her lips, deliciously plump as summer berries, thinned at the edges as she considered. She hesitated, and instead of answering my question, she asked me, "What happened to *you*, Thomas? What secrets are you hiding?" And something within me jarred loose.

I told her everything.

I told her about my skating dreams and the night during the skating competition, when it all fell apart, and how after the operations to repair my knee and shoulder I started all over with another skating partner, and once again how my body abandoned me.

I told her about my Martha, and how the drunk driver survived the crash, got out of his crumbled truck, took a swig from his bottle of cheap rotgut, shattered it on the pavement, took a piss, then walked home. All the while, my dear, sweet, adorable Martha lay mangled, mixed together with all the twisted metal, dying alone on a backwoods country road, with no one to hold her hand.

I cut myself wide open and told Winter *everything*.

⚬

Little by little, as Winter and I found comfort in our conversations, we realized that we had become dependent on our private time together and felt a little lost when we didn't make the effort to catch up on the local buzz.

For me, it was refreshing to have a woman as a friend instead of thinking of her as a conquest—something that seldom happens in my life, but when it does, I sincerely cherish it. And I am absolutely positive, Winter felt the very same.

We never once met outside of our workplace. In a way, that made what we had as friends all the more special. The truth was, after getting to know Winter, I would have never wanted it otherwise. I'm not saying she didn't jump start my heart when I was around her anymore. That was always going to be a constant battle for me.

(What I'm saying is, we found common ground that made our friendship a unique experience. A person simply cannot ask for anything more. They may think they want more, but the truth of it is, having an honest and trustworthy friend is a rare and beautiful thing.)

She asked me a lot of questions about Martha, and my skating, and I was open and honest in the telling. She made me laugh when she thought skating was for girly men doing all that spinning and twirling in the air. But I explained most men are idiots and said to her, "What man wouldn't want to be out on the ice with all those pretty girls in short dresses?"

There were times when Winter wanted me to read her some of the stories I'd written, and because I felt so comfortable with her, I obliged. She was a good listener, as was I, and that all by itself made it easy for us to enjoy our time together over a good cup of coffee.

One day she did something entirely unexpected. She gave me a copy of a drawing that a neighbor drew of her, and of her father when she was a child. I knew it had special meaning, but it wasn't until later that I understood why she'd given me such a precious gift. It was something private and personal, like a love letter hidden between the pages of a book, or inside an old shoebox tucked away on a dusty shelf, brought out to be used when spirits needed lifting. I keep it close to me, folded in my wallet.

❧

The summer washed away slowly, with only a couple of tempestuous thunderstorms that rumbled across the sky. Nothing out of the ordinary for Indiana. And every year, the older I got, the seasons seemed to move along so much faster, and when it came to summer, I didn't mind at all if it moved along as quickly as possible. But that year, it seemed to take forever.

Summertime in Indiana can be profoundly boggy and oppressive, racked by heat and insects, with humidity pouring sweat into your bones. The trees laden, leaves slumped, covered with the dust of the world. The air so sticky and heavy, instead of sliding effortlessly into my lungs, fights its way down. Not like in the spring when the air is so refreshing, invigorating, and sits on your tongue lightly, melting away like flavored shaved ice.

Few around these parts like the summer and most are ready for it to end as soon as it begins. I, for one, was glad to see it finally make an effort to move on and allow a cooler season to take its place.

❧

When Winter decided she could let the ghosts of her past trickle out, it was late October, and a thin cold rain was sweeping through the forest.

I love the fall season when the trees take their last deep inhale before their long sleep. The leaves flaunt their spirited shades of yellows, reds, and oranges, dressing the landscape with splashes of wonderful color like splattered paint on a Jackson Pollock canvas. It dazzles me, lifts my spirit, and ignites a soothing flame of warmth inside me. Earlier in the day, I had heard the unhurried call of sandhill cranes flying south, which reminded me of trumpets in a parade.

It had snowed a couple days before, but the ground wasn't cold enough for it to stick. The wet autumn air carried with it the smell of woodsmoke. It was that heavy, frosty air of an approaching winter that promised to be long, cold, wet, and gray. (Most don't appreciate winter as I do, especially during weekends when one feels free to nap without guilt.)

The chill that spread through the forest that day was typical for October, but not unpleasantly so. Any colder, though, and all the rain would have been snow for sure—which I wouldn't have minded at all. There had been a chilly breeze, which had been brisk, and gusty all day pushing colorful leaves off the trees. There was talk running through the lodge of colder temperatures and a snowstorm moving in from the northeast.

❧

The night before, a couple of bats braved the chill and tickled the pale frosty evening sky as they snatched insects on each pass above my head. Soon they would stay home, snug and warm in their winter hideaway, where the summer's heat and its piggish dog days would become a mere dreamy memory. It was the perfect twilight I love so much, that kind that teases you, flicks your ear, making a pledge of many more lurking around the brisk corners of October.

Yes, autumn with its shorter days and colder evenings had fallen on Brown County.

I gazed at the spangled sky and wondered if people's souls danced among the stars. Or whether they stayed on earth, forced down by gravity, drifting aimlessly, eternally, among the trees in the forest.

I hoped not.

Given the chance to choose, I'd waltz among the stars.

What could be more glorious than to rumba and cha-cha with the cosmos?

❧

It was the end of the workday for me, and I was sitting on the loading dock alone, taking in a long satisfying gulp of the sharp October air before I headed home, thinking of nothing in particular. Just taking a moment to let the workday energy drain from my shoulders, watching the colorful trees toss their branches like hula dancers telling a story.

I heard the bleating call of a pileated woodpecker as it flew. I wondered what tree it would perch on next to peck the life out of the heartwood for a sweet tasty bug; or perhaps it was returning to its already pecked hole for sought-after rest from head-knocking wood all day. I breathed in more of the brisk autumn air, appreciating the chilly edge of it and the scent of fallen leaves. I inhaled one last big, greedy gulp, pulling in any traces of tension left over from the day and letting it out in one long, satisfying exhale.

Simon pushed through the loading dock doors, took a step forward and let the doors close on their own and lit up. His worn-out Carhartt, patched-up dark, gray work jacket was loosely draped over his shoulder. He took a hard pull and said while smoke filtered out of his mouth and nose, "Sure glad it's Friday, bub. Bit chilly, ain't it."

"Don't be loanin' out your truck to nobody this weekend," I said to him as he walked past me and down the steps, taking another drag on his cigarette.

"Why don't ya pick me up Monday mornin'." he said without looking back while putting on his jacket.

"Sure enough," I replied. I watched him walk around the corner puffing away and thought how nice of a guy he really was, and how fortunate I was for having had the chance to know him.

I was about to leave, too, when Winter pushed through the loading dock doors, ready to end her day as well, wrapped in fall. She was wearing a lightweight, chocolate-brown corduroy mid-length jacket and a faded, rusty-orange wool scarf haphazardly curled around her neck, but in fact, was purposely placed to appear chaotic. It suited her well and complemented her red hair, accented with a matching brown corduroy newsboy hat, tilted to one side.

I loved the look. It was understated, yet sophisticated for a country girl, except for her black, slip resistant work shoes. Put her in a pair of thigh-high suede high-heeled boots, and she'd look like she belonged in a fashion magazine, despite her diminutive frame. Her posture was a slight shouldered slouch, and her feet were dragging from fighting gravity all day. It had been a long day at work for the both of us but on the surface appeared to touch Winter more with weighted soul searching.

She hesitated when she noticed me, then walked a few more steps and stopped. Her liquid green eyes met mine with a delicate but precise touch as to be difficult to analyze or describe, but I had a suspicion of what she was about to do. It was a look I've seen many times before. But part of me, though, wanted it to be *that* look. You know what I'm talking about, that look when a woman yearns for more than just friendship.

No, I knew it wasn't *that* delicious, lusty yearning.

It was the look a woman becomes afflicted with when she wants something from a man, but not that *something* a man wants. The reality of it was, I knew the look sparkling in her eyes was merely an echo of a thought still yodeling in the back of my own hankering, lusty heart.

&

I turned away from Winter, lowered my head to stare at the ground, and closed my eyes. I felt as if I could see right through my lids. If I'd had a sketchbook, I could have drawn Winter to the perfect likeness. I could see Winter's soft, natural, rouged lips that need no painting (which knocked my socks off), and how she wears the perfect amount of makeup, so it's difficult to tell if she is wearing any at all. And how her fingernails, although worn from work, were well tended, short, and un-painted.

I inhaled slowly, could feel it expand my lungs.

When I opened my eyes, I looked up and watched her walk straight for me—purpose in each footfall. It was how she car-ried her body and the way her soft curves pushed against her clothes that aroused my senses and made my stomach leap whenever she was near me. In truth, it was more than that. It was more than arousing my inner libido, as opposed to my impulsive cravings, that wanted to do more than just fantasize. There was something almost mystical in her allure. Then again, I was smitten, like a teenager's first crush.

Was I dementedly moonstruck?

Yes.

Nothing I couldn't control. (Okay, maybe tying the pink

ribbon around the book was pressing lightly against the edge of insanity, but I was pretty sure I was past that stage.)

The simple fact was, I cared for her.

Wanted to protect her.

You know, the things a man is supposed to feel and do for a woman unconditionally when they're friends.

⌇

I could hear my breathing was heavier.

I gently shook my head clear. But I couldn't rid my mind of one silly curiosity. *What it would be like to feel Winter's lips next to mine.* I brought my head up and looked directly at her, straight into her eyes, like when cupid's arrow finds its mark, and I could tell she was burdened with years of disappointment. "Hey, Thomas," she said to me, which sounded more like a question than a friendly howdy.

She stood still for a second and looked at me steadily, with a brush of a squint, as if questioning the reason I was still at the lodge.

Her body language said everything.

A favor, perhaps?

No, it was more than that.

She was surrounded by an aura of something mixed with hopefulness and worry, and I saw something pushing against that aura, trying to break free.

So I asked, "What's goin' on?"

"You have a minute?"

She walked over to me and sat down, letting her shoulder touch my shoulder. She placed her hands in her lap, fingers twisted like strands of a lanyard, turned her head to face me, and looked at me again with that same questioning squint. My eyes lingered on the tiny freckles that sat gently on her cheeks and walked softly across the bridge of her nose.

It wasn't difficult to tell she was keyed up.

It was the way she said, *"You have a minute?"*

There was the tone in her voice, a tone I have heard over and over when someone is about to reveal something personal and private. "I have all the minutes you need," I told her. While she had schooled her features to betray nothing from her past, she had little power over the light that had come to her eyes, dark that it was, with the need to tell her story.

I often wonder why people feel such comfort around me to tell me their tale.

Maybe it's my charming personality?

Or my ungodly good looks?

Well, it's certainly not that.

Maybe it's a voodoo thing that surrounds me?

A sixth sense, perhaps? Not in a bad way, but something people feel in a good way.

Animals are the same with me. Horses will nuzzle my neck and push air into my ear, and cats I've never met will curl up in my lap and purr themselves to sleep. I have absolutely no idea why people feel they can confide in me about the secrets they've kept hidden behind closed doors. But they do. And I let them. And I am honored they have trusted me enough to divulge their secrets. My journals overflow with narratives of those who felt the urge to let loose and give up the skeletons they would have otherwise kept under lock and key—all of which were given to me freely, with nothing expected in return. Some of their stories we have all experienced, while others seem like fiction.

One thing is for sure: I am always amazed at the endless fascination and astonishment I have at the unpredictable nature of their stories. Most times people try and starve the nagging hurt that lingers by ignoring it.

When their suffering resurfaces in the telling, with such gaping emotional pain, I have always tried to show empathy, hoping I might give some comfort when their lament pours into the open. At times, they have so much heartache to unload it's more than my simple heart can hold and it feels like a balloon filled with water ready to burst.

⌘

I knew Winter was ready to tell me her tale. But she sat like a statue in silence for such a long time—locked into herself—I was beginning to wonder if she was having second thoughts.

I could see the pain of her past cover her sultry green eyes like a thin, black veil. I knew better than to say anything—and kept quiet. The most painful of tragedies people have pushed aside for years are hard to bring back to the surface. But when someone does find the verve to let the pallid undertone of despair escape the far reaches of their universe, forcing it from them is never the answer, and yet I was eager to learn Winter's secret. I wanted to yank out whatever it was she was trying to keep locked away and place it in front of her so she could let it go. Even so, I had figured out years before that being patient and giving someone a moment to turn thoughts over was always the best avenue to follow.

So that's what I did. I waited. And after a long pause, in which I could only describe as being tentative, I could see her eyes shift into a fervent and long focus as if she could walk right into the past.

And slowly,
Winter told me her story . . .

Winter's Story

Off of State Road 135, about twelve miles north of Nashville, Indiana, farmlands mixed with horse farms lie peacefully in a small valley nestled between rolling hills of thickly wooded forests.

In that valley was Winter's family farm. A proud, two-story clapboard-style farmhouse painted white, with black-trimmed windows and matching shutters. Passed down through genera-tions of iron-willed Hoosiers. Upstanding, assiduous men and women to a fault—traits mirrored in the farm's character and thousands of memories echoing in each room, from the lath-and-plaster walls to the weathered pine clapboard siding on the outside. All the buildings that were built on the farm were simple, efficient structures, traditional in design, not one of which—despite their age—lumbered or leaned. Foundations were as reliable as when they were first laid more than a century before. Eight large oaks and maples surrounded the farmhouse like sentries—guardian angels protecting their outpost—with limbs stretching out over the house like glistening wings, holding back the sun and shouldering snow in the winter. Scattered between, dogwood and redbuds stood together, locked in a waltz that had lasted for decades.

It started out as a small two-bedroom house, built by hand by her great-grandfather, with additions constructed when needed by her grandfather and father. On the west side of the house, a few hundred feet from the kitchen, a matching barn stood tall and solid, crowned with two large, ornate cupolas. The barn opened its doors to acres of healthy planting fields, which now were tawny in the fall, edged by bush clover, wood mint, and a forest thick with oak, poplar, and sycamore decorating a creek.

ཉ ◆ ཉ

Tragedy has a way of touching a person's shoulder with its bony finger of fate, prodding everyone at least once in a lifetime. Tragedy is kind of like lightning and the lottery. It's rare for it to strike once in the same place, let alone twice, but it can and it will—often with destructive force. It struck Winter hard, harder than most. Not once, not twice, but three times.

She told me it took every ounce of her soul to fight her way back. Every day was a battle, and as time tramped forward, her struggle to feel solid ground again became less bleak. Still, even as Winter was beginning to see flickers of light through all the bitter despair, unbidden memories would flood her mind and wake her, and she'd feel like she'd been body-slammed by the weight of everyday expectations. Pushed yet again into the bottomless pit of distress.

Back to the poison.

∿ ♦ ∿

The first lightning strike was when she lost her mother to cancer. Winter was five at the time.

Five years, though, was old enough to keep the pain locked in the veiled recesses of her heart. She remembered four scenes the most—moments that set the foundation for how she protected her feelings even now, pushed them into the dark on the far side of the moon.

First were all the trips to the hospital, especially the last one—sitting alone in a chair in the corner of her mother's hospital room and watching her father kiss her mother for the last time.

The second memory was pressing up next to her father, the acrid smell of his wet cotton trousers, wrapping her arms around his leg as the attendants lowered her mother's oak casket down into the dirt. It was a chilly windy spring day. Raining hard all morning, saturating the ground. The grass bowed and swayed from each gusty blast, and the rain had matted the newly planted summer wheat down to stringy clumps in the farmer's field that bordered the cemetery. Her feet squelched in the muddy grass. She wasn't cold, yet still, her body shook.

Third, the sound of the casket crashing in the muck at the bottom of the pit when one of the canvas straps that supported the coffin broke loose and the heavy thud of her voluminous Aunt Ota fainting on the graveyard green, face up, right on top of her Uncle Will's grave.

And the fourth, when she and her father were walking back to the truck. She turned to look back and saw one of the attendants, on his belly, dangling headfirst into the open grave to retrieve the strap, while the other attendant held his ankles. Memories that reflected like fragile soap bubbles, dreary images, popping in and out of her head for the rest of her life.

∾ ◆ ∾

The second lightning strike happened thirteen years later, piercing her without warning when her father died suddenly from an aneurysm.

It happened a couple of weeks before she celebrated her eighteenth birthday. It was on a sunny Sunday afternoon after church, in midsummer, while her father was inspecting corn roots out in the field. There are moments when the unexpected happens that pushes us back hard—like a sledgehammer to the gut, and when her father didn't come back for lunch, she knew something was wrong. Without meaning to, a person can tip the scales of fate in a different direction, as Winter's father had. Fate doesn't care if a person is alive or dead to change the course of one's life.

She was already hardened to the ache of a broken heart from her mother's death. Her father's death added another clotted layer of sadness; another sign that she was destined to travel the path of heartbreak; another experience that wanted to knock out naïve childish notions of everlasting love, hope, and a bright and happy future.

ॐ ◆ ॐ

For months after her father's death, Winter looked as if she'd been hit by a truck or crushed by some considerable weight.

She told me that when she looked in the mirror, she didn't recognize herself. Her mouth was pressed so that her lips had become thin. Dark skin had formed half-moon bruises beneath her eyes, and her soft features had sharpened unappealingly from loss of weight. She said her arms felt stick-like, and where her work shirt fell open and formed a V, her collarbone looked like the edge of a two-by-four. The image of Winter wasting away was difficult for me to imagine when knowing her as I did, a vibrant, confident woman, sparkling with hope.

There were times where she believed she was paying the penalty for the past sins of her relatives. Whatever those sins might be, she had no idea, but like everything else in her "life," life seemed to crush her, hold her down. It was like falling into an endless flume at the bottom of the ocean floor, frightful and silent, with the weight of the sea above relentlessly pressing down on her body, holding her in place. But in reality, it was what it was. Her father suddenly dying was just another consequence, another lightning strike to leave an open gash which would be difficult to stitch, and, at the time, seemingly impossible to repair.

ॐ ◆ ॐ

The people she loved the most had been pushed away like a cottonwood seed being blown by an angry wind, stolen from her, yanked into heaven.

The loss of Winter's mother and father left furrowed scars so acute that trying to move on seemed beyond the capacity of her broken soul altogether—inconceivable. Some sorrows you carry around as though they are part of you, attached, like your little toe. You don't always think about your little toe, but once in a while—especially after you've stubbed it—you realize it's there. When that happens, you remember there's nothing you can do to forget it, and every pinprick of pain washes over you all over again.

⚬ ✦ ⚬

Winter said to me, she never appreciated just how precious every peaceful moment was with family and friends until it was taken away.

Some calamities stay with you forever no matter how much you try to block them out. When you lie to yourself to protect your hurt feelings, a lie is merely a lie, no matter how hard you try convincing yourself otherwise. Admitting that you're lying, though, is the first step forward in the search for veracity.

For a lot of us, it's almost impossible to fight against the parlous cloud of tragedy when it interjects pain back into our lives. Once we do triumph over it, we can experience the sweet taste of sunshine on our tongues once again. But for Winter, after her mother and father died life felt raw and fetid. And now, all she had left was the farm and all the bills that came with it.

Winter was a determined person by nature, and she continued to work the land as her father, grandfather, and great-grandfather had done before her. But there was, swaying back and forth, and surrounding her, a pervasive sense of tension, urgency, and fear that she had never felt before (stretched thin, almost to the breaking point with anxiety), and a question that hung loosely in the air—what will happen next?

~ ◆ ~

Too many times, though, Winter's grief had become nothing more than another whispered rumor for her neighbors' entertainment.

People tend to talk in small farming communities like Winter's, where it's impossible to make a move without everyone being apprised of everything you do, or what happens to you—even before you know what's happened to you. When a new family was about to move into town, everyone knew who they were, their family history, their ages, and their likes and dislikes, weeks before their furniture was delivered. Having a history in a small town that stretched back generations, as Winter's family did, was a double-edged sword.

On one side, everyone was willing to help out in a crisis— and they always did. But on the other side, everyone knew your personal business. That's what the mores and means of living in a small town are all about, and in a way, that's part of a small town's charm: good neighbors and good gossip. Oddly enough, there was comfort in that for Winter.

~ ◆ ~

Even though some of the townsfolk were willing to help with the farm, they could only do so much, and their support would wane. After that, Winter would have to hire farmhands to help keep the farm running, which meant more expenses, and yet another level of anxiety. She already knew there wasn't going to be enough money to pay all the bills, on top of paying farmhands, no matter how good the harvest. This was a fact she couldn't ignore, but even still, she knew she couldn't work the farm alone. Winter had to hire help.

To offset her worries of making ends meet, she decided to work as a waitress at the local diner, Kathy's Café. Kathy had been a close friend of her mother's, and Winter knew she would be willing to let her arrange her work hours so they wouldn't conflict with the time she needed to work the farm.

ॐ ◆ ॐ

So here was this attractive, intelligent young woman—a simple upright country girl wanting to hang on to her family legacy, running a small farm, working another job in the evening, dreaming of a better life, and dragging herself home every night dead tired from the long days.

She felt strangled by her dreams, tormented by hopeful possibilities of a better life that always seemed like it was running away from her. It felt to Winter as if all her hopes, all her dreams, all she had ever wanted out of life, was sprinting down a winding, foggy country road, turn after turn, concealed somewhere in a misty haze, only inches out of reach.

ॐ ◆ ॐ

Winter loved the farm. She loved its history. She loved how so many generations of her family had lived and worked it—their sweat, tears, and blood enriched its soil, and now hers mixed with theirs, continuing the tradition that gave breath to the land, life to the farm. In return, the farm gave purpose to her world, brought meaning to it, and made her feel worthwhile—especially when the crops covered the planting fields with a faint green haze. Spring was one of Winter's favorite seasons, and she measured its advancement by the flowers, encouraged by some secret encrypted message to sprout.

Daffodils were the first to trumpet in random patches lining creek beds, front yards, and along the roadside. A few tulips had begun to break out, bordering the brick walkway to the front entrance of Winter's house and dotting its perimeter like colorful, magical sprites.

Spread out unevenly all over the farm were tiny, delicate orange and white flowers, which reminded Winter of splashes of butterscotch and randomly tossed miniature marshmallows. And her favorite, buttercups that colonized around the fence of her vegetable garden and provided a pleasant smear of yellow that always brightened her day.

This year's rotation was soybean.

When Winter walked the furrows inspecting the lacy sprouts, she felt like a skiff floating through a calm and peaceful sea. She worked side by side with the farmhands—and it was tough, gritty work—but she grew up with it and loved it all the more because of the satisfying consciousness hard work gave her spirit. And then, after she had spent all day out in the field tending her crop, she'd rush off to Kathy's Café to work the dinner shift.

At the café, she was the waitress, sometimes the cook, and

was always busing tables, cleaning, and locking up. Then it was back to the farm to put the chickens up for the night and finish chores she hadn't been able to take care of earlier in the day. It was touch and go all the time for her, and it took every ounce of strength to make enough money to finish out the year and not break the bank.

For Winter, that was okay.

At least she still had the farm.

And that gave her some peace of mind.

The farm held the collective memories of generations. Her aunts and uncles owned the past, what was left of them, but they had no love for the farm. If they gained control, the land would be sold off and broken into parcels for residential development . . . It was up to her to own the future.

During the days and nights of the lives of each member of her family, from her great-greats to her mother and father, the farm was where any and everything of significance had been revealed around the kitchen table or debated on the front porch. And the farm knew everything about her family. Their aspirations, broken dreams, unrequited loves, births, deaths, all their secrets . . .

It was not like Winter to ever give up hope. She continued to chase happiness. She continued to believe, especially in hope. As if it pulsed within her.

Guided her.

She would never stop working the farm.

It was in her blood.

It was the only life she had ever known.

The only life she thought she would ever want.

The farm wrapped around her like a handmade quilt. It was her center.

> But life is a notoriously fickle animal,
> bouncing from one extreme to the other on a whim.
> The truth of it is . . . well, you know the cliché:
> nothing lasts forever—and it's true.
> Nothing lasts forever.

*Sometimes things just happen
and no matter how much we'd like it to be different
there's absolutely nothing we can do about it . . .*

— Friday, September 06, 1974

I have the weekend off from training.
Working at John Wanamaker's as a stock boy.
Need to pay for extra skating lessons.
On my break.
Wilmington is a nice town, but I don't want to live here for the rest
of my life.
Competition season is upon us.
Training with Bear.
Workin' my ass off.
The new skating partners are perfect.
They are not spoiled prima donnas.
They are dedicated, hardworking athletes, like me.
They have the same dream I have, to be a champion.
We are ready.
This could be the year.
Besides my Martha, I have never wanted anything as much as I
want to stand on the top step of the podium, to raise both arms above
my head and wave to the crowd.
I see it so clearly each time I dream of it.

· · ·

— Monday, November 25, 1974

In a hospital bed sulking.
Dislocated my knee and shoulder during the pairs event at the
Midwest Championships.
Dropped my partner.
She's okay.
I'm not.
That's it for me.
It's over.
Career ending accident.
To have a life (a skaters life) that is inextricably entwined with my
soul, then suddenly amputated, is more than I think I can live with.
Now, what do I do?

· · ·

— Saturday, December 28, 1974

Bear called today.
He asked if I would like to be his teaching assistant.
Not sure.
Maybe.
Need time to heal.
Miss Martha.
Everything falling away from me.

Part Two

CHAPTER 11

The Would-Be Prince

Thursday, January 18
Late Evening: Almost midnight.
The night sky is so crisp and clear it has awakened
more stars than I have seen in the longest time . . .
Had a bag of powdered sugar doughnuts for a snack.

One day, without warning, a glistening splinter of hope became a clear and definite distant light punching through turbulent clouds. She had moments when she was lonely for the closeness of a man. Not often, but sometimes. And when a good man finally brushed against her shoulder, she took it as a good sign that things were turning for the better.

I was surprised when she told me how guilty she felt of wanting to go on a date or buy a pretty dress, or to have a night off to go to the movies with a man by her side, and how much that played so heavily on her mind. Everyone deserves the basic pleasures of life I told her. But like most people, trying to control the yearnings of the flesh is tantamount to saying, "I'll never eat another piece of chocolate." In this regard, every now and then, Winter was like most everyone else; she liked to have something sweet.

ᷰᷧ ✦ ᷧᷰ

Without realizing it, the man Winter met had become a regular thing. They were becoming friends, yes, but it was really more about the pleasant relief to be around each other that helped Winter feel whole again, intact, instead of lingering in a never-ending pool of worry. For Winter, maybe a man was more like a shield protecting her from the heartache that followed her filling the empty space her mother and father had left behind. Whatever it might have been, their friendship worked, and she didn't want to let him go, even if true love wasn't fixed tightly to their hip.

He was just shy of six feet, with thick gold and reddish hair that reminded her of harvest wheat and rust. His eyes were unusual, a light brown color, like coffee with a touch of cream.

Handsome? Yes. In a too-perfect way that makes a man love himself more than anyone else ever could. She said he looked like the quintessential bull rider when he wore a denim work shirt and his Wranglers. So I suspect he would have been the perfect model for a Calvin Klein ad in Vogue or plastered on billboards all over Japan, showing off his delicious round cowboy butt for Big John jeans. She did say, despite his movie star looks, he was a trustworthy man, and forthright, with a good heart, and emotionally stable—or so it seemed on the surface.

That man was Ben.

ᷰᷧ ✦ ᷧᷰ

When Winter told me something that was very personal,

something that only she and Ben would know—as I am about to tell you—she would lower her voice and move closer to me, as if to keep the memory a secret so it wouldn't spoil. She did this often when we talked, inch closer to me. I could taste the strawberry scent in her hair.

I liked that.

Made me feel special when she sat next to me like lovers do.

And each time she did, her voice became soft and I knew she was telling me something that placed a mark on the palm of her hand that could never be erased.

❧ ◆ ❧

Meeting Ben changed her in so many ways. She enjoyed being with him. Very much. And yet, there were times when they were lonely together.

Sometimes, they would spend an evening drinking a couple of cold ones, see a movie, and make love. Each time, after they'd finished their night play and were drifting off to sleep, Ben would say to her: *"You're the best, Winter."* She wasn't exactly sure what he meant, and she didn't ask, but wondered, *Did he mean I was the best girl he had ever met or the best sex he'd ever had? Maybe he thought it was something I wanted to hear or something all women wanted to hear? Maybe he was trying to be polite, and the sex wasn't that great?* It didn't matter all that much to her because, for the most part, she just thought it an odd thing for him to say, and Winter liked being with him, especially when loneliness prowled around inside her.

In addition to his ravishing, billboard good looks, Ben was a friendly, good-natured man, and extraordinarily willing and enthusiastic about helping her around the farm. A big plus for sure. Ben wasn't her one true love, and she wasn't his, but they shared a passion for each other which had grown over time. They were both good at filling the void when loneliness scratched at their ankles trying to add self-pity and despair to their lives. And because of that, they found comfort and security when they were together.

Winter thought maybe in time the respect they had for each other would morph, like a butterfly, and emerge as true love. It's been known to happen, but in this case, she knew it was doubtful. It was more like accepting how things had turned out and saying to yourself, *I didn't expect that to happen, but it's okay. I can live with it.* So she let their lack of real love hang between them, as thin and wispy as the ghostly scent of long lost hope and unfulfilled dreams.

❧ ✦ ❦

Ben was a hard worker, and he shared Winter's worries about keeping the farm, which made it much easier for Winter to deal with the burdens of day-to-day life and all of her concerns that had piled up over the past few years.

They talked about their future, as couples do, and decided they should live together on the farm. And when they found out they were pregnant, they married. It wasn't a whirlwind romance. It wasn't a fairy-tale wedding. It was a quiet ride to city hall and then over to the obstetrician for an ultrasound. But what was also true was the fact that compromise was necessary to have a successful relationship, and beyond wanting to have her baby, she wanted to have a marriage that was happy.

After the doctor told them they were going to have a girl, they dashed off to buy all the pink baby things they could lay their hands on. Plus a few boyish blue items, since Winter wanted her baby girl to be rough around the edges, too.

❧ ◆ ❧

Winter stayed at Kathy's Café as a waitress and continued to help around the farm. Kathy had been a good loyal friend and a shoulder for her to cry on. She took care of Winter after Winter's parents passed away—loving, caring, and protective to a fault. She was tough-skinned, rough around the edges, stocky and spry. Her voice was husky, so she often spoke softly to cut the edge of it. She had a bad hip and limp when she walked, and her hair was thick, once black as night, but now salted with gray.

Kathy's radar was always on around Winter. If Winter coughed, Kathy would quiz her about her health and make sure she saw a doctor. When she had an emotional crisis, Kathy had a tissue in her hand before a tear rolled down Winter's cheek.

It was a comfort to have Kathy as a friend. Important.

It kept her grounded. Made her feel like she still had family to rely on, and she cherished the stories Kathy would tell her about her mother. That helped her keep a connection to her mom and gave her memories she didn't have the opportunity to have as a child, or as an adult.

When it came to the farm, she and Ben kept one hired hand—Frankie—to help Ben. Ben and Frankie worked well together, especially since Frankie had proven to be a steadfast, reliable worker. Always showing up on time and willing to help in a pinch. Her opinion of Frankie was mixed, though. She liked him for the most part, but there had been moments when Frankie made her uneasy. She would catch him glancing at her in the way most men had since she hit puberty.

Winter didn't mind all that much; she was used to being singled out by men and had learned to ignore it. What surprised her with Frankie though, was that she liked his attention and found herself checking Frankie out on occasion, when he had his shirt off, sweaty from work.

I actually felt a little jealous when she told me about Frankie. Based on her description, the man had a healthy, tight body and tattoos covering his arms and shoulders.

A sexy look she said. (If you're the type of woman that likes that sort of thing I thought.) Winter thought it was beddable, though. And when she said the same about his snakeskin cowboy boots—that they were a sexy look—I rolled my eyes. She said to herself, *Nothing wrong with looking.* But she said she never let Ben know she'd been eyeing Frankie. A secret she kept to herself.

In any case, everything pressing down on her was about keeping the farm afloat so she didn't pay much mind to Frankie checking her out. As long as he did his job well, that was all that mattered to her. If his ogling became creepy, she'd tell Ben and let Ben deal with it.

❧ ◆ ☙

After a lot of backbreaking work, Winter and Ben had found their rhythm and wrestled the farm into submission. With Frankie's help, things were moving forward smoothly. No

hiccups that Ben and Frankie couldn't resolve swiftly with inge-
nuity and careful planning. Not only were Winter and Ben able
to make ends meet, they were also able to put a small amount
into savings.

Even though there hadn't been that wash of romance with
Ben, he was a good husband and a kind, caring father. Now,
she had a home and a family, and finally, all seemed as exactly
as she had hoped it would be. But more than anything, with the
help of Kathy, what made Winter find her way back to the living was her baby girl. Chelsea's birth had awakened the mater-
nal love that had been missing in Winter's life after her mother
passed away.

That pure unconditional love brought hope back to Winter.
She felt it the very second the nurse plopped Chelsea on her
belly and Chelsea wrapped her tiny hand around her thumb.
A mother's heart completely melts the first time their newborn
baby stretches out, searching for the one who gave them life, as
if saying, *"Thank you."*

Winter said something to me I have never forgotten—that
Chelsea was, from the minute she was born, a cosmic extension
of her soul, separate, yet connected by an invisible string. I love
that thought. Something I will never truly understand since I've
never had any children.

❧ ◆ ❧

Winter told me despite losing her parents at a young age, her
childhood had been wonderful, and she'd been deeply loved
by her mother and father. Her parents didn't spoil her by any
means. They gave her plenty of chores around the farm to teach

her responsibility and build her self-esteem. "You wuz born on a farm, sweet-cakes," her father always told her. "Right here in this house. That means you gots farm blood in ya, girl. Makes you strong, not like them city girls." And when she was old enough, he'd put on his big daddy grin and say, "Hey, farm girl, git on that tractor an' plow them fields."

And then she told me there were moments after her mother passed away when she would sneak into her father's room and steal one of her mother's sweaters and gently rub her face into the fibers, inhaling every ounce of her mother. Even now, as an adult, she missed her mother's touch. Back then, with her mother gone, there was still so much love in their home that she never felt lonely or deprived. That warmth, that full and contented feeling her parent's had given her, that's what Winter was determined to give her daughter.

◌ ◆ ◌

Ben, on the other hand, hadn't been an only child. He had seven brothers and one sister. His parents had kicked him out of the house as soon as he turned eighteen. He had no distant relatives to speak of and few close friends. "The lost child," he called himself. When they brought Chelsea home from the hospital, the evening air had been cool and the night sky filled with stars. The house had a chill running through it, and as they stood next to Chelsea's crib, Ben wrapped a shawl around Winter's shoulders and held her close as they gazed at their baby girl. Ben admitted to himself that he was in awe of the tiny bundle, shocked too, but more surprised by how Chelsea's arrival had so quickly added the kind of warmth to their home that he'd never had growing up. But it surrounded him with images of his past that he hated thinking about.

Those memories had a way, more often than not, of intruding at the most peaceful and intimate moments he shared with Winter, especially what happened on the day he graduated high school . . . "I bet you figured once you graduated you could just leech off your parents?" his father had said to him. "Wuz that what you wuz thinkin'?" A cold gust had blown across the front yard, his father's threadbare, scraggy open robe flapping like a broken mainsail as he stood on the porch in his loose-fitting, grungy, blue-striped boxers and a stained white T-shirt. *A Spartan soldier preparing to do battle with the Persians*, Ben thought. *Almost laughable.*

But Ben wasn't laughing. Such posturing from his father, Ben never understood and felt he didn't deserve. Sometimes (many times) it ended with a hard slap across the face or a fist to the gut. His father had a cigarette and a bottle of beer in one hand, crumpling Ben's diploma in the other. "Well?—Wuz ya thinkin' you could just live here in *my* house with me an' your mom?" The sound of the wind rustled through the trees. A train blared its horn in the distance. "Answer me, goddamnit!"

"Would it make a difference?"

"Nope . . ." His dad held out his clenched fist with the crumpled diploma, pointing his finger at Ben. "This is just a fuckin' piece of paper—means nothin'—," he pounded his chest, "but it's my fuckin' piece of paper. I paid for it." He stood still for a second and dropped the diploma on the porch. Ben drew in a slow breath. One of his hands balled into a fist. The other hand reached to cradle it. Ben's dad took a swig of his beer and flicked his cigarette into the yard. Another gust rushed through, pushing the diploma down the steps and across the front yard, slamming it into the neighbors dead evergreen shrub.

❧ ✦ ❧

Ben shared the same ambition as Winter; he was determined to give their daughter a home filled with family spirit and affection, a safe haven—something he never had.

Their little girl would never feel like a lost child. They made promises. In the hospital room. Chelsea had been no more than hours old. Winter and Ben's eyes held each other, their voices were firm—through their eyes, through their voices—a promise to protect their daughter and give her a home filled with love, hope, and laughter. A home where she could return to, no matter what happened in her life. If there was one thing about being a family they safeguarded above all others and believed, all the way down to their ruby slippers, click your heels three times . . . you know the rest . . .

❧ ✦ ❧

One of my favorite stories Winter told me about Chelsea, had been when Chelsea was a month away from her seventh birthday.

It was nearly midnight when Winter heard the back stairs creak. Someone was sneaking into the kitchen, and since two other someones lived in the house, not including the three cats and two dogs, that narrowed it down to two possibilities for the creaking staircase tread—her husband, or Chelsea. She reached over and found Ben in the same position he'd fallen asleep in.

Winter smiled and eased herself out of bed, making sure Ben didn't wake, and quietly went down the front stairs (which didn't creak) to the kitchen. She peeked through the doorway and on the kitchen table was the leftover ham from dinner, the mustard, and the mayonnaise jar, lid open. A flashlight balanced on its end, lighting the ceiling and casting a soft glow on her daughter, who was making a midnight snack.

"Whatcha doin', sweet-cakes?" Winter whispered. Chelsea froze. Her eyes grew wide while holding a spreading knife in one hand and piece of bread in the other. Winter let her smile widen and sat at the table across from Chelsea. "You still hungry, huh?"

"Yep."

"Well . . . You were born a farm girl . . . sooooo, you got farm blood in ya. An' that means you get the munchies at midnight an' need to eat a lot more than those silly city girls. All farm girls do—that's what my daddy told me. An' now, I'm tellin' you."

"Are you sure?"

"You betcha. That's an awful nice sandwich you're makin' there." Chelsea smiled back and placed the piece of bread she was holding carefully on top of the other half that was stacked with ham and lettuce, cut the sandwich from corner to corner, and handed one to her mother.

❧ ✦ ❧

Even with the dream Winter had always had (the one she thought was the perfect relationship, the perfect family), their marriage was working—imperfect as it played at times, it was working. Marriage, she believed, should be bound with glue—lifelong glue.

But, there are times when things happen that abruptly alter the direction of peoples lives.

᷾ ◆ ᷿

Ben and Winter had been together for eight years when Ben had a terrible accident. A copperhead snake startled his horse, and Ben was thrown off, hitting his head so hard that he was knocked unconscious for twelve hours. It had been a Saturday. Breezy in the early morning but a clear sky with a few puffs of white hanging in the blue.

"I'm gonna take Whiney an' ride her up over t' the south corner," Ben had said at breakfast. "I need t' check them plants t' see how they're all doin'—I'll be back right 'bout lunch."

"I wanna go," Chelsea pleaded.

"Sorry, short-stuff. Not this time," Ben replied. "It's a long ride. Frankie's goin' with me 'cause we got a lot more t' do than just lookin' at them plants." Chelsea's smile turned sour. She dropped her eyes down to her cereal bowl.

"I tell you what," Ben added as he leaned closer, inches from her ear. "We'll go for a ride this evening. Right here close by the barn." Then he pinched her nose and wiggled it.

"Promise?" Chelsea looked up and the corners of her mouth lifted.

"Promise."

It hadn't been more than an hour later when Frankie came galloping hard and fast into the barn without Ben. Winter threw down her pitchfork and rushed to the truck.

"What happened?" Winter asked quickly. The truck engine roared as Frankie accelerated, spraying gravel in all directions.

"Snake—hissed. Whiney, bucked," Frankie said throwing out the words, sweat beading on his forehead. The truck zig-zagged and bounced on the uneven dirt road, stones pinging off the underbody.

When they got to Ben, his body was lifeless, unresponsive; matted hair mixed with dirt and dried blood. The air was crisp, filled with the aroma of new sweetgrass. Whiney grazed as if nothing had happened, reigns hanging to the ground. Spring peepers chirped in chorus in the nearby marsh. Ben's face was pale, skin clammy, but he had a pulse.

Winter and Frankie picked Ben up and placed him on blankets in the bed of the truck. Winter sat beside him. "Keep his head still," Frankie said firmly, "an' don't let 'em roll 'round."

Winter's throat was dry, her tongue thick. She braced herself, her upper body on Ben's chest, legs pushing against the truck's wheel well to hold him still. Her hands gripped his head. Her body ached, and the rush of cold spring air from the racing truck pounded her.

Not again, she said to herself. *Please, not again.*

❧ ◆ ❧

I was amazed at how vividly Winter remembered that moment, and how her posture—like a tic beneath the eye—would stiffen in the telling, and she'd pick at her cuticles. The fear. I could almost taste the scent of it. Sticky and sour.

She told me that sitting on the chair in the hospital room, next to her unconscious husband, brought back all those hated memories of doing the very same with her mother. The IV, the beeping monitor, the dull light coming through the window. The echo in the room when talking. The buttery, creamy yellow on the walls. All of it, bringing forth the baneful images she tried so hard to let go of. But the worst nightmare was thinking how Chelsea might have to live a life without a father. She couldn't do it again. Couldn't. Wouldn't.

"He's going to be fine, Winter," the doctor said right after the surgery. "We were able to reduce the swelling. He's healthy and strong, so his recovery should be pretty quick, but he's going to have one helluva headache when he wakes up."

As soon as Ben was released from the hospital, he had to go back, complaining of headaches. The doctor reassured them that the headaches would fade with time.

But the headaches didn't stop. Ben didn't recover.

He became dark. Brooding.

They returned to the hospital for more tests. But the results were negative. Every scan, blood sample, and coordination test came back showing that absolutely nothing was physically wrong with Ben. They were told the same thing as before: that the headaches would diminish over time.

Ben tried to do the farm work like he did before the concussion and spend a full day tending to all the chores. But he couldn't. On a good day, the best he could do was work only a few hours. Winter was thankful Frankie was there to pick up the slack.

❧ ◆ ❧

It broke my heart hearing Winter talk about how Ben drifted toward the dark side. From all that she told me about Ben, it wasn't difficult to figure out what might happen to him, because, as Ben marched further into the dark, he became increasingly withdrawn. As if someone had reached inside him and switched off the light, switched off the Ben whom she used to know and respect.

Passion, affection—any loving feeling Ben had for Winter evaporated, and when she reached out, his lovemaking felt more like an obligation, instead of the lawless sexual appetite he'd always had for her. Ben burst into rages triggered by the most ridiculous things—the saltshaker wasn't full; the spoons were spoon-side down in the dishwasher. His moods created a capricious climate, strange and disturbing. At times darkly menacing.

Some days Ben would be entirely rational, the man Winter knew and respected. And then there were days where the entire universe revolved around him. He would be in such good spirits that it made everything singularly unmanageable. Cheerful to the extent it seemed fake, forced, unquestionably out of control, where he wanted to buy a new tractor for the farm—even though he knew they couldn't afford it—or drive up to Indianapolis and eat at a fancy restaurant. And when she didn't appreciate his high spirits, it would piss him off. He would rant and rave like a spoiled child.

The episodes of euphoria were the strangest, and in a way the most alarming, because it had become her signal that Ben was about to click off like a switch and return to the darkness. When that happened, a poisonous cloud would cast its shadow at the back of his eyes. He'd sulk, hiding in the guest bedroom for days (covers pulled up to his chin) or spend hours sitting on the edge of the hayloft or disappear into some hidden hollow around the farm till long after sunset.

"What on earth are you doing up there navel-gazing?" Winter said to him once when she found him in the hayloft, head in his hands and feet dangling over the edge. "C'mon down from there, Ben. Horses need pickin'—somethin' you didn't do at all last week, an' you didn't do it yesterday. Now they've got so much mud in their hoofs they're limpin'."

"I'll do it tomorrow," Ben said absently.

"I also need you to get the tractor up an' runnin'," Winter continued, ignoring his lack of attention. "I want us to finish plowin' under all the corn stalks before we lose the weather— you said it might be the starter, or spark plugs, or somethin'."

"Tell Frankie t' do it." Ben stood up in one quick motion, body tensed, ready to spring.

"C'mon, Ben—what's the problem?" Winter tried to say in a soothing way. "Jeez, Ben, I need you right now."

"Shit, you don't need nobody," Ben yelled, slamming his fist on the railing. He took a long, resonant look at Winter, raised both arms, and regained control, and said in a quieter tone, "You know how t' fix the damn tractor. Frankie can do it. I don't care—I want to be left the fuck alone."

⁓ ◆ ⁓

Winter tried to talk rationally to Ben about his dark moods, but he'd never say much. The times Ben didn't get completely lost in his woeful, brooding world, was when he played with Chelsea. Then, he was fully engaged, completely attentive, head

over heels for his daughter. Laughing. Loving. Tender. During
those quiet moments, Ben seemed like the man Winter had
married. She desperately wanted to do something to help him,
but everything she tried aggravated the situation, intensified it.
It got to the point where she gave up. Didn't want to help him.
All she wanted to do was protect what little sanity remained
in their marriage. When she tried to get Ben to see another
physician, it elevated his erratic moods, and he'd storm out of
the house yelling, "Quacks! They're all quacks."

He spooked her. He was so not there. Each time she tried
talking to him, he'd answer—sort of—so concealed somewhere
else in his head that she wondered if maybe he needed to be
committed or something. Just for a while. And having those
thoughts made her feel so disloyal that she couldn't face him,
or at least that's what she told herself.

Winter once said something to Ben that she regretted:
"Ben, there's something hidden inside you that worries me so
much. You frighten me . . . and I don't . . . I don't think I can
help you. I don't think I *want* to help you."

His moods made her feel like her family was being stretched
like an accordion, layers, and layers splitting apart. The world
around him was veiled and dangerous while her world seemed
to shrink, and she feared she would suffocate in its smallness.
Yet, she had this vague hope—a very vague hope—that somehow, Ben would beat the demons that were egging him on.

                                          ≈ ◆ ≈

Winter's lightning strike with Ben happened early in the
morning. A spring morning. The air was brisk but not too cold.

In the months of April and May, Ben had been too lost in his dark world of despair to work on the farm. It was Winter and Frankie who raked the earth, plowed and planted for the summer and fall harvest.

Winter loved spring when the newly planted seeds—precious little ones that pushed through and hugged close to the ground—sprouted from the recently turned earth and reached for the sun. A peacefulness floated among the trees. An untroubled sense of promise as she watched the baby plants spring to life. Working the farm in the spring, especially during the cooler mornings, connected her to something greater than herself, carrying with it the hushed whisper of hope and tranquility, with nothing unusual placed upon it.

Not that spring morning.

Within the tranquility, an ominous cloud had formed, prickly on the skin, like the flu giving a hint of the sickness to follow. It soaked into Winter's pores. A muscle ache she couldn't figure out. A strange sense of instability hanging in the air. Heavy. Prevailing. So much so, Winter's neck and shoulders shivered to reduce its influence.

An early morning misty rain had brought with it a thick fog moving with undetectable determination toward the farm. Winter stood by the kitchen sink and watched the hazy cloud silently prowl along the ground, making a foggy path toward the barn. She watched Ben go inside, and her uneasiness grew, and she thought, *I'm being paranoid?* Then she thought, *Maybe, not?*

Winter opened the kitchen window and let the fresh morning air flood in. It brought with it the perfumed scent of new growth, wakening trees, everything that leads us to spring fever and the urge toward happiness. Robins and sparrows, she noticed, were having a heyday out in the field for an early morning feast, no doubt pleased to discover that the newly turned earth had lured worms to the surface.

A benevolent hand had been poised over the farm all morning, protecting it from the surrounding storms; rumblings and lightning strikes had rolled on in the western horizon. But the air was soggy and thick with moisture, ready to burst open and spill out. Like a sponge needing to be squeezed dry.

Typically, she, Chelsea, and Ben would make breakfast together when Ben was feeling well enough to help. But there were times Ben would completely disappear in the early morning—leaving without a word. Watching him go into the barn gave her some worry, yes, but at least she knew where he was. And when Ben had moments like this, it was better to distance herself. Anything she'd say to him when he was grappling with his dark side would set him off. So she made a mental note to walk with careful steps, and keep herself on guard.

᷎ ◆ ᷎

Earlier that morning, Ben had said to her with a quiet, dusty voice, "We had a coyote kill a couple of chickens last night." He stared vacantly out the kitchen window while washing his hands, and added, "Death is a messy thing." He paused, wiped his hands on his jeans, turned to Winter, pulled her gently to him, leaned back against the sink and said, "I'll be in the barn." His fingers weaved through her hair and held the back of her head while his left hand caressed the length of her spine. He kissed her on the lips. Barely touching but lingering for a second. Then kissed her ear, and whispered, "You're the best, Winter." Winter's entire body tingled.

The kiss was sweet, gentle, the way she loved to be kissed by Ben, which had become infrequent since the accident. She missed that. Missed it more than she ever thought possible.

҂ ◆ ҂

Winter hadn't thought much of it when Ben told her that some chickens had been killed. Each year they would inevitably lose a couple of chickens to a raccoon, fox, or coyote. It's part of living on a farm. It was the way he said, *"Death is a messy thing,"* that was difficult to ignore. It was his tone of voice that seemed misplaced, odd, dour. And the kiss, although pleasant, didn't seem right, unfinished.

While Ben's toffee-colored eyes on his good days would kindle with warmth and understanding, they were lifeless that day and filled with a much broader sense of torment after the kiss, as if preparing for one of his dark moods to return. And his smile . . . it seemed crumpled, more like an apology.

҂ ◆ ҂

Chelsea was upstairs getting ready for school. Winter cleaned the last breakfast dish, placed it in the drying rack, rinsed her hands of suds, and yelled, "Chelsea! Get dressed and get down here!" Then, shaking water off her hands, she added, "The bus will be here soon. Hurry up, sweet-cakes." She heard Chelsea's muffled reply in the background of her mind and stood motionless, staring out the window, not really looking at anything, more like looking past everything, when a strange sensation pushed through her. Like a wisp of a thought when entering the mind that leaves so quickly, it's lost before ever having a chance to know it. But it leaves an imprint. It's something undefinable, and yet, it was a pressing feeling she couldn't set aside.

Her eyes refocused on the barn where daffodils, tulips, and wildflowers carpeted the ground like colorful dancers at a concert. She dried her hands on the hand towel, wiped the excess on her jeans and threw the towel onto the edge of the sink. She put on a light rain jacket and reluctantly stepped outside. The sweet scent of honeysuckle hung in the air, and a red-tailed hawk soared and screeched above the trees, on the prowl for breakfast. She looked up at the bird, its white underbelly a stark contrast to the gunmetal gray clouds, and watched as it swooped down into a tuft of ryegrass, pinning its helpless prey.

The crisp, fresh spring mist sprinkled her face as she walked with guarded steps to the barn. She heard the hawk screech again and then listened to the call of its mate. She looked at the two birds circling and catching air. For a moment, as she watched the birds floating with the currents, gliding side by side, swooping, lifting, switching positions—she closed her eyes and could almost feel the updraft. She put her ear against the barn door. Opening her eyes as if to listen better, she hesitated, inhaled a shallow breath then struggled for another, not sure if she could actually open the door.

It was quiet, like pond water on a hot summer day, still and stagnate. Not even a rustle of the horses in the stalls. *Too quiet,* she thought. *Ben must've let 'em out to pasture.* A tremor of dread flashed through her, a foreboding shadow. She tried to shake it loose, but couldn't.

It was in the air. On her skin, oily and slick.

She sensed it. Felt the blackness of it.

The first groundswell of real fear.

The hawk screeched.

She flinched.

Her heart was saying to stay away from the barn. Get Chelsea and walk to the bus stop. But her head was saying, *I have to know.* And the rest of her body was fighting between her head and her heart, making her feel like a screamer in a horror film who's creeping down the steps into a dark basement, while the audience is yelling run away.

Winter bit her lip and tightened her fingers on the door handle and slid the door open, just enough to let herself in. A scream froze in her throat, her face flushed with heat, yet at the same time, the rest of her body disconnected, cold, frozen. *This can't be happening,* she thought. *This is not real.*

But it was real.

Her husband was suspended in midair with a rope around his neck, hanging from one of the beams that had supported her family's barn for over a hundred years.

Time became elastic, stretched out in all directions . . .
Sounds turned into muted accents . . .
Colors shifted to gray . . .

❧ ✦ ❧

Winter placed her hands to her mouth and muffled the scream trying to escape so Chelsea wouldn't hear her panic. The adrenaline pumping through her body made her legs ache from the effort of standing.

She was lightheaded. She leaned forward, using her other hand to support her weight on her knee, rocking her upper body side to side, hoping the rhythm of the rocking would be of some comfort. Winter tried to swallow, couldn't, and tried again. She gagged, doubled over, then retched, though nothing came out.

She straightened herself up, but her knees were spongy. The look on Ben's face engulfed her, smothered her, and hit her with a force beyond physical. Spasms tore at her body, forcing her to lean over again. She braced herself, bent forward, and put her head down, hoping she wouldn't faint.

Another wave of spasms struck her. She sank to her knees, head still bent over with her hands on the barn floor, clutching straw thinking: *this isn't happening.* The barn seemed to shift and swirl around her. She shut her eyes to stay the swirling, which had become like a blurry photo. Blackness descended on her, filling her gut with cold, dreadful pain. Her inner voice ascended to a terrible, eldritch wail that became so strong she had to clap her hands over her ears.

Then . . .
She felt the inexorable pull to open her eyes . . .

ॐ ◆ ॐ

The horrible angle of Ben's broken neck and the tortured grimace on his dead, motionless face, seared into her retinas.

His lips bloodless and blue.

She was transfixed with a mixture of horror and sympathy.

She gulped more air in, and the world started to sort itself back into order, the dusty barn air, horses, bridles, and halters hanging by the horse stalls. All the pieces fitting together. The bittersweet scent of manure and hay. Her husband's feet floating above the ground. His soiled trousers.

She put her hands to her face, pulling down on the skin along her jaw, savagely pulling, saying nothing, thinking only, *Oh my God, Ben, what have you done.* She closed her eyes again, unconsciously clenching her fists. She let the tears pool, blurring her vision before spilling out, flooding her cheeks. Suddenly nothing below the waist had any feeling. The barn was going black. It was shrinking, shrinking to a single bead of light—darker, darker. From that bead grew a sound, no a voice. A small voice as if lost in a thick fog, "Mom! Moo-oom, where are you?" Hearing Chelsea's voice felt like a hard slap to the face, instantly forcing Winter to clear her mind.

Reality rebooted.

She placed both hands on her face turning in the direction of her daughter's call.

When she looked toward the open barn door, everything was still out of focus. She moved toward the door, like an underwater diver in a strong, cold current. She stopped. She panicked for a second, worried Chelsea would walk in and see her father's lifeless body and her mother drowning in tears. Her pulse jumped into a gallop. Blinking to clear her vision, she wiped the tears away with the palms of her hands and rubbed the wet stains from her cheeks.

She looked at Ben once again, but only vacantly, raked her trembling hands through her hair, then brushed her jeans clean and rushed to the barn door.

She peeked out around its edge, like a frightened hunted animal, and walked out of the barn, watching Chelsea coming toward her. She wiped more tears from her face, closed the barn door behind her, pushed her fingers through her hair again, and walked toward Chelsea, pretending like nothing had happened. Her breathing evened out.

"Hey, sweetie," she called out, keeping her voice calm and steady. Without missing a beat, she reached out both arms and scooped Chelsea up, balancing her on her hip, and moved down the driveway—away from the barn—to the bus stop.

"Let's get you to your bus on time."

"Where's Daddy?" Chelsea questioned, rubbing the last bit of sleep out of her eye as she waited for an answer.

"Daddy—well—," Winter hesitated a beat before she regained her composure and said, "You know Daddy. He's always got somethin' to do around here." She tried to control the tightness in her voice and keep her legs from melting away. She added, "I bet he's out in the fields lookin' at all the new baby plants."

She gave Chelsea a hurried kiss on the cheek. Chelsea smacked her lips, making a muffled pop for her kiss back. Chelsea slid off her hip and skipped to the end of the driveway searching for the school bus. "Hey," Chelsea yelled over her shoulder. "Don't forget to remind Daddy he promised we'd practice barrel racin' tonight after dinner."

Winter stood by the curb, detached as if standing in the aisle of a movie theater watching a scene being played out on the big screen. Long shot of her baby girl stepping onto the steps of the school bus. The camera panning behind Winter while Chelsea turns around and waves bye before entering the bus. Close up of Chelsea smiling. Happy. Then cut to Ben hanging in the barn. It all seemed to her like something someone had written in a screenplay. And she, Winter, was merely an actress caught inside the story, with no escape while the scene unfolded before her.

Back At the Lodge With Winter

Winter's ability to recall such powerful feelings and clear images continued to mesmerize me. Her posture, the look in her eyes, the tone of her voice—it was as if she had transported herself (and me) to that very point in time. But she had me hooked the minute she began telling me her story hours ago.

I was sure she wasn't finished yet. Nightmares like those don't just burn or scorch the surface, they sear profoundly and blacken the skin. But I honestly didn't know if I could deal with more emotional stuff. It was wearing me down. I felt like I'd been dragged shirtless over rough wood. But Winter was my friend, and I knew she needed to let out the stale air—to the very last breath.

When I reached for her arm, I squeezed it gently. She flinched like I'd yanked her out of the past, back to the loading dock. Back to now. I asked, "How did you stay so calm?"

She turned to face me, exhausted from the telling. Her eyes were filled with hurt, and the lines running from her nose down to her mouth showed the stress she'd placed upon herself from reliving the memory. She rubbed away gentle tears, but could not stop them. My own heart was splitting apart. She dropped her head down, wiping her hands on her thighs. I rubbed the nape of my neck, trying to ease my own stress, wanting desperately to hold her in my arms.

I heard what I thought was a squirrel searching for an acorn in the newly fallen leaves, but when I looked toward the noise, a raccoon raced off with some spoiled lettuce it had found next to one of the trash cans. When she lifted her head, I had time enough to see that her eyes had become red-rimmed. I felt a pang, but I didn't stop her. She brought her lips together and opened her mouth to sigh. Her voice heavier now, weary. I listened as her words broke and wavered from that awful memory when she said, "I *wasn't* calm. The one thing on my mind was gettin' my daughter to the bus on time." Then she told me. "I was so *fuckin'* angry." She paused, rubbed her eyes again, and added, "I wanted to kill Ben. Isn't that crazy. I thought if I'd killed him—with my own hands—it'd make sense."

She also said she couldn't sleep for more than a few minutes at a time for months. The barn, her husband, the black body bag, the ambulance—everything about that day—played in her mind like scenes from a Shakespearian tragedy, making their entrances and exits, depriving her of rest. Even today, she said there are times those images haunt her and wake her in the middle of the night. A silence sidled between us that held us together yet kept us apart. I don't know what it's like to have a close friend or a family member commit suicide. I did, however, know something about the sting of death, when the love of my life had been taken from me. The pain is excruciating; it pierces through you, it clings to you. It's the night without the dawn, it's a breath without exhale, it's all these things and more. I tried to say something to her, but all the words I thought were appropriate seemed wrong, caught between my mind and my mouth, hovering aimlessly at the back of my throat.

The truth of it is, some memories can never be deleted.

∽

The big, burly dishwasher, Ash, must have dropped a couple of dishes. Winter and I flinched at the muffled crash of heavy glazed ceramic breaking into noisy shards. The rain had stopped. Menacing clouds girded over treetops but were breaking apart. The sun poked through crevices, like angels descending from heaven, splitting the soft sunset light into amber-cast rays that spilled out in different directions and found a place to rest on the loading dock.

A wash of déjà vu hit me hard. My mind derailed for an instant, bewildered, confused, believing she and I had walked this path before. The sound of dishes breaking, the golden sunset, Winter wearing her rust-colored scarf. I could swear I had already witnessed that moment. The sounds, the smells—all of it. This happens to me often. It's disquieting, and each time it stimulates my senses; uncontrollable cold waves roll along my spine. The nape of my neck tingles. My shoulders shiver. I float out of my body, forced back the instant I leave.

I sat still, swimming in the unblinking silence, trying to

recapture my déjà vu, thinking of all that she had told me, and contemplating the dancing twilight. For a moment, I was poised between daylight and darkness. Hypnotized by the soft golden light making ghostly snake-like waves on the loading dock entry doors that was slowly fading, and what remained of it were shadows that created wells of emptiness.

I moved my gaze from Winter, taking in a considerable breath and felt my lungs expand until I couldn't capture any more air. I held it in and let it fall out of me the second I noticed a spider's desiccated corpse in one of the upper corners of the doors. It hung loosely on a wisp of tattered web and swayed back and forth in the draft from the frisky October breeze. A thought jumped into my head that Ben's life seemed as futile as that bit of dirty, beaded silk the spider had released in the last split second of its death spasm. Not an epiphany of any sort, just an odd correlation of images my mind put together the minute I saw the dead spider hanging from its wispy thread. Winter pushed into my awkward silence and asked, "You okay?"

"Yeah, I'm fine," I replied. Then I said, "It's a lot to take in." The thing was, I couldn't stop thinking about what her husband had done to her, about the spider, about life and death and all that we leave behind.

"You want some coffee?" she asked. Her voice was kind, soothing, and the rims of her eyes were redder than before. She placed her hand on my shoulder, rubbing gently, consoling me instead of *me* consoling her. She stood up and looked down with her big green eyes and said, "Let's get some coffee."

Most of the time, I would melt when a woman would look at me the way Winter had just then, but my mind was still caught in the web of her husband's suicide.

"That's a hell of a thing, about your Ben." My own voice took that tone of understanding reserved for a friend who is dealing with such genuine soul-searching and loss.

"Yeah, a hell of a thing," she echoed absently. Then she shook off whatever effect my words had on her. "He really messed up."

Actually, "messed up" hadn't been the expression Winter used that night. I must confess, one of the many things I liked about her, besides the fact she had brains (for a cute country bumpkin), liked the opera, and liked going to museums, was that cussing fit her like a well-worn pair of tight-fitting denim jeans. Despite my obvious attraction to her, I never like using expletives except when I'm by myself, typically when I'm driving. Generally, I don't enjoy reading profanity in books, especially when the f-word is used obsessively. Using that four-letter word is offensively coarse and unnecessarily reaching. It's just plain primitive in real life. However, there are situations where swear words are a quality that is inherent to a person's nature.

That I accept. Winter was that kind of person. She used strong language. It was part of who she was—a farm girl who always competed with the best. Maybe she thought the words gave her strength, empowered her. But when she said *that* cuss word, it didn't sound so out of place. It rolled off her tongue like any other word.

I'm not fucking kidding you.

⚜

I got up, and walked over to the loading dock doors, and held one open so Winter could go through first, still partially lost in the image of the dead spider swinging back and forth on its web. "Sometimes things happen, and there's nothing we can do about it," I said. "Sometimes we just have to live with it, I guess."

"I guess." She walked under my arm and through the door as the dissipating sunlight danced on her shoulders. "Thanks."

I followed, not sure if her "thank-you" was for holding the door or for taking the time to listen to her story. Perhaps both.

As she passed me, she folded her arms pulling her jacket closer to her. No question it was getting chillier, so coffee was a perfect idea. Having coffee always reassures me that everything is right with the world. In a way, one might say coffee is a good cup of commiseration. Well, that and hot chocolate, or a good shot of whiskey.

❦

As we entered the kitchen, Ash had a broom, sweeping up broken dishes. Others rushed around, ignoring the shattered mess, and preparing orders. I enjoyed the energy of the night shift, even though I rarely worked at night. Plus, Natty worked during the day. A good thing for sure. Made me grin. I wished Simon worked the night shift so Natty couldn't cause trouble and take advantage of him. I gave myself a reminder to talk to Simon in the morning about working nights more often.

Winter and I walked over to the nook, and as she poured coffee into a takeout paper cup her hands were trembling, ever so slightly. "Ben left a note," she said as she handed me the cup of coffee and poured one for herself. "All he wrote was—," she hesitated, taking in a short breath and letting it out quickly. Then started over. "All Ben wrote was 'I'm sorry'—nothin' more. Just, 'I'm sorry.'"

❧

Instead of returning to the loading dock to continue our conversation, we took our coffee and weaved through the restaurant, working our way to the back lawn of the lodge. Around us swirled the hearty voices of hungry diners that rose up and joined the energized atmosphere and food-scented air—a baby's fretful wail, rustling silverware, whispers, and laughter of patrons engaged and enjoying their evening meal.

The last fingers of sunlight, diffuse, the color of honey, streamed through the inner courtyard garden windows and lit the restaurant, spilling off tables and falling to the floor. The buffet overflowed with fried chicken, roast beef, breaded tenderloin, mashed potatoes, green beans, and hush puppies, creating an aroma that mixed and merged their scents into a flavorful, tantalizing redolence that made my stomach groan.

The lodge had a reputation for its good-ole country-style home cooking. I thought I'd get something to take home later, but for now, coffee would suffice. Then we passed through the adjoining banquet room, which tonight was used for dinner overflow. We sauntered out onto the back porch of the lodge and were greeted by its rolling view of the unspoiled wooded scenery looking east. The evening was dissolving quickly into darkness, turning the surrounding forest into silhouette.

On the way out, I saw Simon and was surprised he was working the night shift and said, "I was just thinkin' about you.

Why you workin' tonight?"

He replied, "I need the moola, bub."

"You know," I said back, "Natty doesn't work nights."

I borrowed his Bic lighter so I could start a fire in the fire pit. Unlike Natty, I promised I would return it to him later, and for some reason, I wondered how many Bic lighters Simon had lost to that voluminous witch. Every time I think of Simon, I think of Natty and how she uses him as her personal toy. I gave myself another reminder to stop making that association. It only added more weight to my worry about Simon and added fuel to my dislike toward Natty.

It was wasted energy about something that wasn't my business in the first place. Then again, I have a knack for doing and saying things I shouldn't.

❧

I had restocked the woodshed earlier in the day—one of the numerous ancillary duties of mine as the set-up guy. Nothing like a warm fire to soothe the soul and reduce the discomfort of reliving a restless and painful memory from one's past, I told Winter.

She smiled and didn't respond.

We planted ourselves in gray, weather-beaten pine chairs, placing them close to the fire. A much more pleasant and relaxing place to sit and talk than at the loading dock next to the grease pit and waste containers.

Winter wanted to keep telling me her story, which was good because I didn't want it to end. But for measurable moments in her telling, her face grew stony in its contemplation, and her eyes turned as opaque as the early evening, slate-gray October sky. During those moments of apprehension and seemingly unending pauses, I patiently watched for her eyes to regain their beautiful emerald hue. That's when I knew she had found her way back to me.

I always find that I am a little surprised how my perception of a person reshapes itself once they give way and open their heart and soul. Even the density of the air seems to change in the telling, filled with the heady fragrance of the unexpected. I sipped from my steaming cup, taking in the acrid aroma and keeping my eyes glued to hers.

I watched her reach back to the memory, and I let her take me with her.

∽

Ben had pinned his note to the ladder leading up to the hayloft.

She admitted to staring at it for the longest time before reading it. It wasn't that she was afraid to read the note she said. "Then, what was it?" I asked.

"It wouldn't change anything—as far as I was concerned my life as I'd known it had ended. How the fuck would a note make any difference. What could he possibly have written that would make it okay to jump off the hayloft and snap his neck? She hesitated and added. "I didn't want a note. I wanted my husband back."

I thought to myself, *It's virtually impossible—most of the time—to stop some things from happening, especially those that are heinous.* She leaned back in her chair, tipped back her coffee cup with both hands, steam rising, and savored the warm sip. "Thanks for stayin' an' listening," she said. The fire let out a loud pop. She turned her head toward the sound.

"I'm happy to listen," I replied in a soft tone.

Still looking at the fire, she said, "Ben's note was written on one of my Christmas thank-you cards. It had holly leaves decoratin' each corner. And a drawing of a snowman wearin' a cowboy hat that was too small for its head, with a carrot for a nose, an' a red plaid scarf... It was wavin' its little crooked, bony stick arm an' sayin', 'Howdy, y'all', like the world was a perfect place." She looked back to me. The corners of her mouth turned up into a weak smile. "Silly, really." A tear rolled down her cheek. She wiped it with her palm. "Ben liked it."

⨀

Winter had sent the cards to friends, thanking them for Christmas presents her family had received the year before.

It was the last card in the pack. She thought that ironic.

Not that it meant anything. It was just odd to her.

We often find ourselves looking for clues that will comfort us when someone we know passes. I got up and placed more wood on the fire while Winter spoke. "I thought maybe Ben used the card, instead of an ordinary piece of paper, because he knew how much I love Christmas—how peaceful it makes me feel." Her face relaxed and the furrows smoothed from her brow. She looked at me asking for understanding.

"Does that make sense?" she asked.

I told her, "I don't know . . . I guess it does if it makes you feel better," My heart understood that Winter would never know why Ben took his own life, and then I added, "Maybe in a way it's better not to know the reason . . . maybe that knowledge will wound the heart more than ease your emptiness. For all anyone knows, Ben might not have used the Christmas card as a symbolic gesture at all. Maybe the note was just a note. And Ben used it because it was convenient."

Unconsciously she held her hands as though she were holding Ben's note, rubbing her thumbs and index fingers and feeling the weight, the texture of it. Another uneasy moment elapsed, and pressing her fingers together, she steepled them, placing them against her lips, closed her eyes, and went on to say, "I sat on the ground, leanin' my back against the barn door. I remember the hardness of it . . ."

My heartbeat had increased, and the scent of woodsmoke from the fire became stronger. I closed my eyes and listened to Winter's voice. "My knees were curled up to my chest, an' I wrapped my arms 'round my legs . . . I just sat there on the cold, wet ground holdin' the note. I didn't care that my ass was gettin' soaked . . . Thomas, I didn't care about anything . . . an' I prayed for it all to be a horrible mistake. I thought if I could cut a deal with God, Ben would walk out of the barn, pick me up an' hold me in his arms. He'd push my hair back from my eyes, an' say, *You're the best, Winter.*"

⚜

The image of Winter leaning against the barn door, curling up in a tight ball, wrapping around herself, spread out in my mind, gray and dense. I could see the breeze tug at her red hair. I could see the note held loosely in her hand. I could smell the fresh scent of the spring mist in the air. I could see her hands clasped together in prayer.

I suddenly realized she'd stopped talking. I opened my eyes. Hers met mine. She wasn't calm. She seemed agitated and shook her hands and cracked a couple knuckles. A rasping, bubbling laugh escaped her, accompanied by a mixture of incredulity and confusion, followed fast by guilt. "I was so fuckin' numb," she said, "I couldn't do anything but wait for the sheriff to arrive and think about that stupid fuckin', god-damn snowman an' his stupid little cowboy hat, an' his stupid snowman smile, an' his stupid, 'Howdy, y'all'."

Her hands fell into her lap as if all the strength flowed out of them (as if she'd dropped the note), then she slumped back into the chair and knitted her fingers together. "I went inside the house and dialed the sheriff. I mean, shit, what else could I go do."

And so she waited . . .

Winter: Losing Ben

᭡ ◆ ᭣

Winter said when she was leaning her back against the barn door, shivering from the cold rain, she kept looking at the note, over and over, thumbing it, and asking herself, *Why? Why did this happen? Why?* She wanted more. Not just "I'm Sorry," but something more. A reason. An answer. But it was just a stupid thank-you card with Ben's handwriting saying *I'm sorry*. She ran her hand through her hair, gathered a handful of the wet, stringy mess and pulled it over her shoulder, examining the ends. She needed to use conditioner she decided and would do that later when she showered. Then, she reached back to the moment when she had told Ben she couldn't help him with his problems. She questioned herself for her insensitivity and felt even worse for not trying harder to help him. Ben was gone. Gone forever. It was then she discovered an entirely new depth of what it was to be alone. For the first time in her life, she felt abandoned. Gut-wrenching, deep-down, helpless, naked abandon. She had never been so utterly alone.

≈ ◆ ≈

Even though the rain had momentarily stopped, clouds continued to blanket the sky, making everything as dark and heavy as the uncertainty closing in on Winter.

The chilly breeze murmured through the trees like a soul in pain as it reached inside her, tugging, pulling her down. If I had known Winter when she lost Ben, I would have told her that those, like Ben, who can't beat away the demons that feed on their souls, will always find a way to end their pain, no matter how much we wish it otherwise.

She thought, *Shit! Why didn't I see it coming? How could I have been so blind?* She knew she would always question herself. *Could I have stopped it from happening?* She had no tricks up her sleeve to cover up the shock of that day. She just didn't know what to do next. She tried holding back her tears but couldn't. Everything let go. Titanic sobs, wave after wave, pounded her, and she let it happen—no restraints—until nothing was left to spill out.

She took one last, tenuous intake of air with a shudder and let it out, hoping to subdue a little of the hurt, even for a second. But the pain remained.

～ ◆ ～

The rain began again, soft, suspended somewhere between a mist and light drizzle. It brought with it a fog that made the day feel even gloomier, thick and damp, adding even more weight to the worries crashing her consciousness: the gossip, the funeral, and especially having to tell Chelsea about what her father had done.

For how long Winter sat in silence she didn't know. Didn't care. Forty minutes at most she thought when off in the distance—breaking into the silence—came the sound of sirens. They grew louder and louder as the vehicles approached the farm. As soon as they turned onto the driveway, the sirens stopped, and the silence returned. It was the crunching sounds of gravel beneath wheels that made Winter regain her focus and momentarily set aside her worries as two sheriffs' vehicles and an ambulance rolled up to the house, splashing through mud puddles that dotted the drive, easing their way toward her, toward the barn. Everything moved in a slow arc as if she had been drugged, but not drugged enough that she couldn't sense the reality of it all. And yet, at the same time, she couldn't feel anything. Didn't want to feel anything. *Things like this happened to people on TV or in newspapers,* she thought. *Now, I'm one of those people.*

All she wanted was to hide from the world and let the day slip away unnoticed. The paramedics were professional and respectful. The Sheriff she'd known her entire life. It was good to have someone she knew take charge of the gruesome work of dealing with Ben's body—as he had done with her father.

The Sheriff was a giant bear of a man, kind, and understanding, with sharp piercing eyes. She wasn't looking forward to the questions she knew he'd be asking her. Mainly because she had no idea why Ben had killed himself. No one is ever prepared for the formalities one must undertake when confronting death. But she had been through it before and knew the order of things that had to happen next.

⮞ ◆ ⮜

The moment the ambulance started its engine to leave, Winter walked away. She'd walked a couple of steps before she stopped, turned, and watched it roll off the drive onto the main road, hitting a pothole, splashing dirty water in all directions, and covering the side of the ambulance with a washed-out, muddy smudge.

She heard spinning tires lose traction on the wet pavement with a sound like despair. The screech intensified her fragile frame of mind, made her shoulders pinch, and she imagined the black body bag lying on the gurney. She shivered from the thought. She folded her arms across her chest. Why that image planted itself in her mind, she didn't know, but it brought her back to what was real, what was happening, really happening.

Ben was really dead.

❧ ◆ ❦

Winter didn't know how long she had been outside in the cold grayness of her shattered day as emotions continued to pound her, but it seemed an eternity.

She closed her eyes and tilted her head up to the washboard, gray, cloud-covered sky to let the raindrops shower her face. It started raining harder, large heavy pelts, and all she could think about was wishing she could bathe the day away, scrub off all the bad. She let the wetness saturate each and every pore. Rivulets ran like veins down her neck. The cold caress of the rain against her skin wrapped around her. A chill ran down her spine and skimmed the length of her arms, moved along her waist, and swirled around her legs. She wiped at her cheeks, brushing off tears she thought she'd finished shedding.

Abruptly, like an afterthought, the rain subsided, and for a moment it seemed as if the clouds yielded to the sun as patches of light fought their way through the dense covering. But the storm clouds thickened quickly, curling in on themselves, silently colliding and rapidly filling the occasional ruptures in the mantle, preventing the isolated pools of weak light from finding their way to the ground.

One honey-colored beam of sunlight, though, found an opening through a small rent in the clouds, illuminated the barn, casting an eerie glow, but lasting seconds, as if highlighting the event that had happened within. The dulcet light faded as a chilly wind stirred Winter's hair and drove the black anvil clouds over the open, tiny seam—angry, heavy clouds—pushing back the sun.

Winter wondered if Ben thought about Chelsea before he jumped. Did he hesitate? Did he question what he was about to do? Did he even give them a second thought? She wondered how a rope would feel around her own neck. Would it feel scratchy? Would it burn when it tightened? Would she hear the bones in her neck snap before everything went to black?

In the distance, lightning forked across the rain-filled plumes, followed by growls of thunder, which echoed all around Winter, gathering its strength, preparing to strike with greater force. The rain started again, light and scattered. The rawness of the air crawled over her. More thunder rumbled. Then hefty droplets of rain came down all at once, and seconds later, the clouds let loose a volley of stinging rain. She shivered, soaked head to foot, and every puff of air felt like a fresh blast of ice. Winter held her jacket closer to her, like a sleepwalker, and went inside the house. She staggered up the stairs, her movements clumsy, entered the bathroom, mindlessly turning on the shower, and let her clothes fall to the floor. She wanted the water hot. As hot as her skin could handle.

The next thing she knew she was in the bedroom naked, water dripping on the floor and standing by the unfolded clean clothes she'd left in the laundry basket, wondering what she was doing staring incoherently at a pile of washed clothing. Her robe. That was it. She'd come into the bedroom in search of her bathrobe. She shoved through the clothes till her hands came into contact with terry cloth, but it was Ben's robe, not hers. She put it on, saying out loud, at the end of an exhale, *What, now.* After that, she ended up in her daughter's bedroom and sat in the chair where she'd rocked Chelsea to sleep when

Chelsea was a baby—still wearing Ben's robe—drying her hair with a bath towel.

❧ ◆ ❧

If sorrow had a face, Winter wore it with keening lines etched openly on her skin. Outside, the full force of the storm raged with violent waves, soaking the farm. A sudden gust of wind rattled the casement like an unspoken accusation, and more lightning flashed and streaked across the sky. She counted the seconds until the rumble of thunder began again.

The pain pushed through her, raw and sharp, with a jagged edge. She gazed out the bedroom window, transfixed by the storm, trying to force her mind into a solid straight line, thinking of nothing but the coming and going of thunder and lightning. But she could barely keep a thought save one, her daughter. All she could do, yet again, was wait. That waiting, however, for the school bus, had been, by far, the hardest thing she had ever experienced.

The storm broke apart, but the clouds remained, readying themselves for another burst. After the bus arrived, she and Chelsea sat on the porch. She kissed her daughter on the forehead and turned her head to blink back her tears.

But the tears came anyway.

❧ ◆ ❧

Chelsea saw her mother as a robust and leap-into-action mom. Sitting on the porch, seeing her super-mom look like a tangled mess was shocking enough.

Chelsea almost never saw her mother cry. Her mother had always been sturdy and indestructible, like a rock, but not this time, and Chelsea let her mother's tears mingle with her own.

Winter knew she had to tell Chelsea the truth because somebody—at school or in town—somebody would say something. Sooner or later, gossip would find its way back to Chelsea. It was bound to happen.

Between tears and quavers, she told Chelsea what had happened to her father and tried as best she could, under the circumstances, to pull herself together. Her tongue felt thick as she answered her daughter's questions. For the longest time, they sat on the porch, crying, holding each other, and rocking back and forth.

✦

Winter had taught herself, ever since her parents passed away, a stoical acceptance of suffering. But when she thought about the most essential part of her, the part that kept her centered, the one element that gave color to her days (her daughter clutched in her arms), it was more than she could deal with, and all her pent-up feelings burst out. She'd been through difficult days before and thought she was prepared to deal with any emotion that barged in unannounced. But she wasn't prepared for anything like what had just happened.

I knew exactly how Winter had been feeling. When the door swings wide open for fear to join with regret, and for despair to gather and simmer with anger, well, I know this evil. I've tasted it. Exchanged blows with it. I still brawl with it. All those sensations together generate unstoppable, clutching surges of anger mixed with regret—more emotions ripping through a person than anyone ever thinks possible.

Yes, I knew precisely how Winter had felt.

❧ ◆ ❧

As the rain tap-danced lightly on the porch roof, Winter looked through it, out toward the hillside along the pasture of her family's farm, thinking of her mother and father, and how, by their deaths, they had dictated the direction of her life. And now, Ben had done the same.

Her mind swirled with new worries. She had to keep her daughter safe and maintain the farm. More than ever, they needed their home to give them some semblance of stability and safety. And she thought how it would mean more hours at the café, again working the farm on her own, hiring another farmhand, and fighting for every penny she made.

At that moment, with all those responsibilities whirling inside her head, she didn't want to think about any of it. She needed to hold her sweet, beautiful little girl and feel her warm body next to her own. Holding Chelsea, feeling her warm skin, smelling her, listening to her heartbeat, that was real. That was life. That, she couldn't live without.

The wind started to howl again, gaining strength, sweeping the trees, pushing more storm clouds that scudded over the farm, unleashing another barrage of pelting rain, saturating the ground, and swelling creeks. The day fell into shadow, adding more foreboding to the already ominous, cloud-covered sky. A peal of thunder marched away to the east, then more lightning and thunder as a murder of screaming crows flew over the barn.

❧ ◆ ❧

When Winter put Chelsea to bed that night, she gazed at her daughter's sleeping face, so peaceful, so innocent, and with such delicate little girl features, breathing so softly while dreaming. When she stretched out beside Chelsea on the bed, she closed her eyes and let the tears wash out as she whispered a simple prayer in Chelsea's ear in hopes that Chelsea would hear it in her sleep. A few moments later, Winter drifted away from the horrible eclipse of the day as she gave way to the unyielding pull of utter exhaustion.

❧ ◆ ❧

Winter had never been sure about her everyday life with Ben because of his mood swings.

She wanted her daily life back from before Ben had his accident, where she'd wake up, make coffee, send her baby girl off to school, work on the farm alongside her husband, and get a hug from the ones she loved when they came home. And no matter what, those whom she loved would love her forever, without question, unconditionally, until she took her last breath. That, she believed, was something everyone deserved; something everyone was entitled to: *Unconditional love. Unrestricted happiness.* Something a family was supposed to have—the life she'd hoped for. It's the life she knew she deserved. Winter had thought, in the beginning when she and Ben were married and had Chelsea, she was living that life.

Ben had taken all that away.

He took more than that.

He took away his chance to watch his daughter grow and become a woman. He would never see Chelsea's first prom, or walk her down the aisle, or hold his grandchildren in his arms. He would never be able to share all the special moments in his daughter's life, and Chelsea would never be able to share those moments with her father.

Winter was angry with Ben for being so self-centered. She wanted to let that bad feeling slip by as quickly as it had tried to make a stand, but she couldn't. Winter was right. Ben had been selfish, very selfish. And foolish. And he had ruined two lives.

He took the easy way out. Devastating those who needed him most. Placing a burn mark on their skin forever. No different than if Ben had hit Winter in the face. Hard. Leaving a bruise she'd never forget. The injury would heal of course, but the scar would remain, buried, hidden, raw. She was prepared to spend many waking days and sleepless nights walking hand in hand with bitterness, instead of trying to forgive Ben for what he had done.

∂ ◆ ∽

As life moved on, days blended into each other without color, and Winter fell into a limbo where it seemed like time had moved on without her.

Family and friends passed on their condolences, and when asked what happened, she couldn't talk about it. To talk about it meant she'd relive it, and living through it once was horror enough. But she still lived through it—the days and weeks and months of it—and when her grieving had lessened, she wanted nothing more than to forget it had ever happened. Some days were better than others, but for the most part, nothing seemed right. Everything sloped; tilted at an awkward angle. Working the farm was the most difficult for her, especially when she had to go into the barn.

Once while spreading fresh hay in the horse stalls, her mind had a sudden flash of her great-grandfather hand-hewing and setting all the timber for the barn. The image unsettled her for an instant: *What would he think if he knew my husband had taken his life using one of those beams?*

The memory of Ben hanging, face ashen, neck broken, had pushed through her like a driverless train barreling down the tracks, out of control. Nausea rushed in; the sweeping, unstoppable violent surge of pain returned. When it subsided, numbness surrounded her, left her enervated. She tried to set it aside, but it bothered her and flashed off and on the rest of the day, cafard images splintering the light. But it made her see clearly that her grief wasn't going to go away easily, and blame was not going to soften quickly.

She was drained physically and exhausted emotionally. It was a somnolence she had never been conscious of before. It sat under her eyes, hidden beneath her skin, putting feverish pressure from her temples to the bridge of her nose, making her eyelids, eyebrows, and forehead feel heavy; a hulking weight hanging between consciousness and unconsciousness, a weariness that never stopped, a fatigue like no other, so powerful not even drug-induced sleep could quench it. Like a discarded, unwanted toy, tossed in the garbage—a doll being kicked over and over again, getting the stuffing knocked out of it, stitching ripped apart, stuffed in a box and thrown in a corner of the attic.

※ ◆ ※

All Winter wanted to do was curl up and sleep, and sleep. Despite her exhaustion, she was preparing herself for the monumental task of keeping the farm from going under. There was absolutely no way she could do everything on the farm with one hired hand. Frankie kept telling her it would be okay. That he'd take care of everything and for her not to worry.

But Winter did worry and hired extra help.

Even taking on another farmhand, she had just enough money to pay bills and the merest trifle for savings. She did the best she could under the circumstances. The one saving grace, though, was always her daughter. When she and Chelsea were together, all the stress of the day bounced off her, and she made sure they both found laughter again to help soothe their troubled hearts.

※ ◆ ※

There were many moments—that came in waves—days and months after Ben's funeral when Winter thought she had stitched some of her ragged wounds together, but the grief would tear the sutures apart, and the pain of all that had happened would gush forth threefold.

She knew marriages started with hope and optimism, love and yearning. But for some, the years together take their toll, and people change. Or in this case, a husband that fell into the dark. What hurt her the most, though, was the pain she felt for her Chelsea, who thought she couldn't be heard at night crying. But Winter heard every single broken-hearted whimper; the raw, biting sobs that would echo in her mind forever.

≈ ◆ ≈

During the worst of those times—after she'd watch Chelsea get on the school bus—when the hurt would bear down on her, she would go to the church she had gone to as a child to admire the light coming in through the stained-glass windows. She would soak in the silence, hoping to find a moment of peace and renewal.

One such time, the candy-colored light scrambled all around her and danced on her skin like a kaleidoscope. She looked up at the stained glass, and spoke in a whisper, "Please, help . . . give me something? Please, anything." It hadn't been intended as a prayer, more like a plea, to help take the pain away with the hope of sweeping some of her fears away, too. Mostly she was attempting to place a bid on hope to put an end to the questions that repeated in her mind. Asking a higher power for answers was comforting.

Each time she made a visit to her childhood church—to dip herself in the placid tenor of the silence—it gave her a brief intermission from her sadness. It gave her comfort and made her feel that maybe one day she would have an awakening. Not necessarily a spiritual one, but a revival that would show her a way out of the dark and grant her passage into the light.

Often though, it was the night that made her anxious. Very late at night, she'd wake and her worries, the desolation—all of it—seemed to get darker and rougher around the edges, replaying that one horrible snapshot of Ben when she found him in the barn.

The one thing that made bedtime tolerable was that she was thankful for any excuse to climb into Chelsea's bed. Being alone in her own bed, where she fought the sheets and blankets at night, the one she and Ben had shared, was more than she could handle. Ben's scent lingered everywhere. His shaving cream. His clothes. It made her feel empty. Lost. Alone.

She swore the walls of her bedroom were watching her. The walls that held the ghosts of all those before her who had lived, made love, and raised children in her family's farmhouse. And now, they captured the memories of the life she and Ben had given each other. It haunted her. And for the longest time, each effort Winter made to try and sleep in her bed, she couldn't. But curling up alongside her daughter to let the blissful cave of sleep overtake her helped most of the time to push back the fears that bloomed at night. Feeling the beating heart of her daughter became her private sanctuary; the place where she found peace. It was then that she could dream her secret dreams, reinvent the adversities of her past, and create a new and beautiful future for her and Chelsea. As long as she had Chelsea next to her, she could quell the disjointed ramblings that raced through her mind, if only temporarily, to help suspend the suffering.

❧ ◆ ❧

Spring was almost over; blossoms that loaded tree branches were being replaced with buds for the next year, fields had been planted showing signs of green, birds protected their eggs and gorged on feeder seeds. Then spring rolled into summer, and summer gave way to fall; fields were harvested, squirrels stored winter food and made their leafy nests, and the sandhill cranes flew south where warmer days awaited them.

And when the winter season brought its first covering of white, it also brought a solitude that Winter and Chelsea took advantage of, to spend quiet, wistful time together, selfishly guarded time, for healing.

❧ ◆ ❧

And so it went, Winter and Chelsea moved in and out of each month like unattached spirits searching for answers and a place to rest. Sadly, even when Winter and Chelsea's life started to budge itself in the right direction, and the healing process began to take shape, simple pleasures continued to fight against the ugly tension of worry about the future. It would take more than a few months for them to feel even partially whole and find a renaissance with life again.

Winter made every effort to visit friends, take her daughter to movies, and go someplace fun for dinner once in a while. Going out and trying to have a normal life helped, but there were some moments that would emerge and descend heavily on her when the loneliness crept back in. And yet, she still carried the hope that one day she might find a someone she could share a life with, a person who would be a good partner and best friend.

A someone she could fully trust.

A someone she could catch dreams with.

It is something I believed she deserved.

Something we all deserve.

one life
one try
one choice
no rewind
no do-overs
no time-outs
one life . . .

— Monday, January 01, 1979

I've been coaching skating so much, it's burned me out.
Not going well being Bear's coaching assistant.
We had a slight altercation. It involved a woman. Bear's twice my
age . . . and the lady, well, let's just say we'll both get over it, eventu-
ally. Lost a lot of respect for him right now.
Need to get away.
Decided to stop coaching and leave Delaware.
Very unhappy . . .

———————

— Friday, June 29, 1979

Arrived on Nantucket yesterday (renting a basement apartment
on Plumb Lane just off of Main Street), and I am already looking for work so I can stay around this quaint whalers village for a
while.
I feel I have walked back in time. I need to get to know this place.
There is magic here . . . I can feel it . . . it dances on my skin . . .
I wish to bathe in its magic waters to stitch the hole in my heart and
stop the pain that seeps from my soul . . .

● ● ●

— *Friday, March 26, 1982*

My time on Nantucket is almost at an end.
It's been an incredible two years. I have taken thousands of photo-
graphs. Can't wait to get into a darkroom and process them.
I have an idea for three Nantucket photography books.
For now, I'm leaving this charming, beautiful island and putting
rubber to the road once again, to see where it will take me.

———————

Excerpt from the author's journal, On The Road.

— *Midnight, Tuesday, August 03, 1982*

New Mexico.
Following Route 66.
Between Santa Rosa and Moriarty.
Flat tire. Truck sitting on the side of the road. No spare.
On my way to somewhere . . . no idea where somewhere is.
Pitched my tent.
For now, I'm enjoying the night show of the Milky Way.
The stars are so thick and bright I have to brush them off my face.
The beauty of the night makes me yearn for my Martha,
the sweet taste of her lips,
and the warmth of her body next to mine.
I will miss her till the day that I die.

CHAPTER III

The Toad

Sunday, January 28 — Early Morning: Breakfast.
Had Egg in the Middle of the Toast.
Something my mother taught me and her mother taught her.
Later today, after writing for a few pages,
I will walk down to the bottom of the ravine,

sit by a tree, and wait to see what wildlife will greet me . . .

After Ben died, Frankie made it a point to stay on the farm as often as possible, usually making up excuses to hang out long after his workday was over. Winter told me whenever she looked back on it, she believed Frankie had it all planned out the minute Ben hired him to help work the farm. She figured Frankie thought if he tried to be her knight in shining armor—always around when she needed someone during the worst parts—the sooner she'd fall for him.

And the sad truth of it is, Winter was right.

Maybe Winter found Frankie attractive because Frankie was the absolute opposite of Ben. Ben was the good-natured guy before he stepped into the Twilight Zone. And Frankie, well Frankie, he was the bad boy. Looking in from the outside, maybe the attraction to Frankie had been born out of desperation and the fear of being alone. It's impossible to know.

❧ ◆ ❧

In the beginning things were okay with Frankie, as it had been with Ben. But Winter and Frankie found they were like two different forks in a raging river, one always fighting to be stronger than the other. It is never simple what brings a man and woman together. It looks simple enough on the surface—hard body and cute ass—but it never is.

There were measurable moments when Winter wanted to choke the life out of Frankie. One might say her relationship with Frankie was more like sticking your finger into a light socket. Something you'd try once, but would never try again, no matter how compelling the temptation might be. It was only later that she realized how clearly delusional she was to have gotten involved with a man like Frankie and to have lost so much of herself. There really wasn't any way to explain it: her fears, his deception, their mutual needs, or their unspoken beliefs about how each partner should be to the other. In the end, there was only what happened.

Hindsight is a distasteful shrew. It is when you wish you had turned left at the signpost, instead of right.

❧ ◆ ❧

Once again, as with Ben, her relationship with Frankie wasn't about falling in love. In reality, she didn't know how she felt about Frankie. She didn't know how she felt about anything. Finding love, she believed, was beyond her grasp. For Winter, love had to be unconditional, unpredictable, and unexpected. Except to say, that love can also, at times, be unbearable, and Frankie had decidedly become unbearable, which had nothing to do with love.

Frankie wasn't a classically handsome man like Ben. His face was rough. Good bone structure, but hacked or rough-hewn, cheeks pockmarked from childhood, which lent itself well to his tough-guy biker image. His nose looked like it could have its own mailing address. Charm he had plenty of, and a sexy, caveman look that made women believe all of life's heavy lifting would be taken care of. His eyes were aquamarines, the palest clear blue. Mesmerizing. And when he smiled, a perfect set of pearls sparkled.

∾ ◆ ∾

When Frankie was hired as one of their farmhands, he thought to himself then, *All I need to do is be the good guy. The always-on-time guy. The helpful guy.*

As a kid, Frankie had worked on farms that surrounded Seymour, Indiana, where he grew up, only a few miles south of Columbus, and Nashville, Indiana.

Frankie's father was drunk most of the time.

When he wasn't drunk, he was drinking.

A distinction that was confusing to the neighbors but understood by Frankie and his mother. Drinking meant his dad's behavior was somewhat under control, sipping a few beers with a loose tongue and biting words but no overt acts of aggression.

Drunk meant Frankie found a place to hide in the house or ran to a neighbor for safety to get away from the razor strap. Being somewhere else when his father had too much to drink was always the smarter choice, rather than waiting for his dad to add more scars to his battered childhood.

The times when Frankie's father was cold sober, the preferred state, the man actually acted like a dad and would play catch with him or knock a soccer ball around. But those moments rarely happened. Maybe, if he was lucky, once or twice every few months he'd be able to hang with his old man, but never longer than a half hour before his dad would say, 'Hell, kid—shit. Fuck this! I need some suds." Then his father would sit on the porch where he wanted to be left alone to drink and smoke while Frankie would carefully sidle off to one of his hiding places where he had a stash of comic books, in case the drinking turned into something more than just drinking.

He thought he'd been luckier than most kids with parents who were drunks because his father left when he'd entered junior high school, left him and his mother without a word.

Just took off.

Frankie never heard from his old man again. He had no tears to shed when his father left. He hated the man. And as he grew older, that hatred grew with him, making Frankie look out for himself and making sure any relationship he happened to be in would always be something he could control and profit from—never trusting anyone.

Frankie didn't have a high school diploma. He'd quit school as soon as he'd gotten his driver's license and took off. Exactly like his dad, except he told his mother. Leaving to be a truck driver, he told her.

Not till years later, hauling scrap iron through Indiana did Frankie realize how much he missed his home state and working on a farm. He was tired of driving all over the country, bouncing from one town to the next. That's when he'd stopped in his hometown of Seymour to visit his mom and read Ben's want ad in the local paper for a farmhand.

❧ ✦ ❧

As Frankie was driving up the long gravel drive on that bright and sunny day and saw Winter's farmhouse and barn standing like they were brand new, he knew he was taking the job, no matter what. He had a sneaking suspicion it could all be his if he played his cards right. He decided right then and there his trucker days were over.

"Are you Ben?" Frankie had asked with a wide-open grin as he jumped down from the cab of his big rig, landing with a crunch on the gravel, sure and steady, like a cagey junk-yard cat with his hand outstretched. "You gotta nice place here."

"Have you ever worked a farm?" Ben asked right away while shaking Frankie's hand.

"Yup. Been 'round farms off an' on all my whole life. I was no bigger than a katydid when I drove my first tractor," Frankie shot back, putting one hand in his back pocket and the other on his truck, patting it to make a point. "Me an' Betsy here—" Frankie said as he rested his foot on the chrome cowcatcher that jutted out from his truck's bumper like a set of buck teeth. "Well, hell . . . we're done haulin' stuff 'round the states. Heck, we've been wantin' t' stop truckin' for some time now. Kinda

wanna make a stand in the heartland, know whatta mean—
miss bein' on a farm—workin' the land." Frankie's smile
widened. "Once dirt gets on-ya, it's hard t' shake it loose, know
whatta mean?"

Frankie's relaxed manner and confidence resonated with
Ben. He liked Frankie. "Well, we got plenty of work for ya, if
you're willin'." Winter was walking out of the barn, finished
with laying down fresh hay for the horses, her red hair sparkling
from the sun. Ben waved her over. "This is my wife, Winter—
Honey, this is Frankie."

"Howdy, Frankie," Winter said with a bright smile while
extending her hand. Frankie took off his baseball cap and put
on a smile so broad, Winter could swear she'd caught the fragrance of toothpaste.

"Ma'am—I sure like your farm."

❧ ◆ ❧

Frankie had artifice and subterfuge written in plain English across his forehead. For Frankie, love with a woman was
all about control, ownership, and what he could get for himself. Greed was encoded in his DNA and taking advantage of
a woman's hunger for love was the perfect way to get what he
wanted.

He had a constitutional weakness for all women and was
permanently incapable of fidelity and labored under the il-
lusion that every damsel was eyeing him. In Frankie's mind,
being with a woman was no different than having one piece
of apple pie, and a minute later trying the cherry, and an hour
after that having a slice of mincemeat.

As a hired hand, he turned out to be one of the best
Winter and Ben had hired—more than capable of picking up
the slack when Ben was caught up in his black moods. And so
understanding of what Winter was dealing with during that
dreadful time. So helpful in fact, she depended on Frankie to
do almost everything around the farm.

And Frankie took advantage of it.

Frankie made sure Winter saw him working. Made sure she
saw his muscled physique, tan and tattooed on each shoulder.
Two winged lions—royal insignia—a regal reposed animal on
the dexter, the right shoulder, like a heraldic shield, and a
wild roaring lion flying through flames inked on the opposite
side, the left shoulder, the sinister side. She remembered what
Kathy had said to her one evening when they were locking up
the café, *"Frankie's dangerous, Winter. You watch yourself. That
man wears sinister as if he'd been born with it."*

Frankie's eyes, although beautiful, were untrustworthy—as
if permanently fused in a half squint. His tongue was coated
with silver, a natural born con man and mild sociopath. And
before she realized it, she was under his spell. "Trust me," he'd
say with a wink and a toothy, cunning smile. "I'll take care of
everything. You need to grieve and heal yourself." The color of
his eyes and that smile, combined with Winter's fear of being alone, hypnotized her so that she never saw his pockmarked
skin and large Cyrano de Bergerac profile. All she saw was a
man she had hoped would ease her pain. And all she heard
was, "I'll take care of everything."

꙳ ◆ ꙳

It was apparent Winter's anxiety about the farm, not to mention her fear of living alone without a man, superseded rational thinking about what type of man she wanted stretched out next to her at night.

At the onset of their relationship, Frankie seemed no better or worse than any man she had dated. Which as we all know, is typically the case when a love tryst is blooming. And when Ben had first hired Frankie, he seemed like an honorable person. He treated Winter so nicely in the beginning and appeared to be genuinely concerned for her when Ben died, but now she thoroughly regretted that Ben had hired him. Even back then there had been those uneasy dust specks of suspicion floating in her mind, instincts, really, that had warned her this was not a good man. Not to mention Kathy's warnings of Frankie's sinister side, a wild roaring lion tattoo flying through flames on his left shoulder. Which now seemed apropos to the actual nature of the man. But she had turned a blind eye to those feelings and now lived with a man who stifled and manipulated her.

ଛ ✦ ଛ

Frankie took over all aspects of the farm—hired two more farmhands—and convinced Winter to apply for a loan, using the farm as collateral. All of which made her work more hours at the café. What little revenue she made from the farm, plus all of the income from the café was paid out to Frankie and the three other farmhands.

Frankie even convinced her to put her father's property up for rent, with the promise they both would find better jobs if they lived closer to Indianapolis. "We can use the rent money an' a percentage of the harvest t' make a better life for ourselves," he told her. "Trust me."

That inner voice banging around inside her head told her not to trust him. But he coaxed her to the edge of a hot iron skillet, and she crawled in like a lean slice of bacon, sizzling and spitting until it was burnt. In the end, she had been the one who got a job when they moved to Indianapolis.

ঙ ◆ ঙ

The transition from life on a farm to living in a large city was difficult for Winter. She tried to adapt, but she missed the unhurried pace of a small town. Yes, living in Indianapolis had some advantages, but not enough to convince her that life in the city was better than life in the country. The house they had rented was okay but in great need of repair. It was built sometime in the 1920s with a second story balcony that dipped a little too much to one side. What bothered her the most was that it stood in a long row of similar houses that were a few feet apart from each other, sitting too close to a very noisy street. Almost no privacy. Every time she used the bathroom she was sure her neighbor could hear her flush.

She dreaded sleep. Almost every night, she would have vivid dreams. Most were short, disconnected, nightmarish vignettes about Ben or ugly disjointed arguments with Frankie. Both of which produced weighty notions of despair, leaving a trace of bitterness that clawed at her senses.

One night after she'd tucked Chelsea into bed, Winter stretched out on the couch in the living room to read. Frankie was not home. Out drinking with his biker buddies, as he did almost every night. She hadn't turned three pages in her book before she drifted off into one of her dreams.

She was back at the farm with her parents.

It was a beautiful, sunny, summer morning. Winter and her mom and dad were gathered around the kitchen table. The hazy morning sunlight streamed through the kitchen window, and everything it touched had a fluffy or frayed texture to it, casting a fuzzy glow around the edges. Her mother was standing, rolling out a piecrust. Her father was sitting in a chair on the other side of the table, cleaning and cutting strawberries for the pie.

In the dream, she saw herself when she was five years old, standing prim and proper by her mother's side, and playing with a smaller rolling pin, rolling out dough, imitating her mother.

Ben and Frankie stood next to the kitchen sink talking uneasily to each other, gesturing with angry motions, pointing at each other, and poking each other in the chest. Ben was holding a rope that had worked its way up and over his shoulder, wrapped twice under his armpit like a snake, then slithered around his neck. The loose end dangled down his chest, rapidly shaking back and forth, making the warning sound of a rattlesnake.

Frankie had an unlit cigarette in his mouth and a bottle of beer he gripped at the neck with two fingers with his left hand. He wore a black, short-sleeved T-shirt, with the left sleeve rolled concealing a half-used cigarette pack. His black and gray tattoos that covered his arms seemed to melt into the sleeves of the T-shirt making it impossible to tell where the shirtsleeves ended and his skin began.

Ben caught Winter's eye, raised one eyebrow, and shook his index finger at her in an accusatory way. Like she was a child who'd been caught sneaking cookies from the cookie jar. Even though she was in a dream, every experience she had ever had, all her deepest secrets, desires, wishes, every emotion continued to course through her. She could feel everything.

Her regrets. Her pain. Her anger.

Winter knew precisely why Ben shook his finger at her. *How could he,* she thought. *Blaming me for his death.* Her cheeks blushed crimson. Her eyes narrowed. She walked toward Ben, prepared to kick him as hard as she could. As if knowing what Winter was thinking, her mother put a calming hand on her shoulder to cool the anger. It worked, Winter looked at her mother, and they smiled at each other. She missed having her mother around and the mother-daughter connection that came with it. She missed how her mother always seemed to know what she was thinking.

She missed that a lot.

Frankie, on the other hand, was following Ben's lead, also pointing his index finger at her, with a mocking smirk plastered across his face. She wanted to crack Frankie's shins, too. She slapped the rolling pin into her hand, hard, like a prison guard's truncheon, gritted her teeth, squinted, and stared directly at Frankie smirking back. But as soon as Winter twitched a muscle to move toward Frankie, her mother once again held her back. This time putting a hand on each of Winter's shoulders.

"Such nice boys, Winter," her mother said, leaning close to Winter's ear, not letting Ben and Frankie out of her sight, and whispered, "but which one's yours?" Winter tried to explain to her mother, but her throat tightened, and she was unresponsive. In unison, Frankie and Ben flipped their hands around, arrogantly showing their middle fingers, and winked at Winter.

Frankie took out his lighter, lit his cigarette, and took a long hard pull. He leaned his head back and let out a long series of perfect smoke rings that grew larger in size as they lifted in the air and evaporated, then he sucked in another drag.

"They're so cute, aren't they?" her mother said, as she gave a quick wink back to Ben and Frankie. Then she added, "It's obvious they like you, dear."

It infuriated her that she couldn't tell her mother what had happened to Ben and that Frankie was a complete idiot. She was becoming hysterical when suddenly—in the way dreams have of shifting from one place to another—she was no longer in the kitchen with her mother. The kitchen had disappeared, and she found herself standing inside the barn. She was still holding the rolling pin, thumping it into her hand over and over. But now, she was an adult drenched from the chilly rain.

When the cold wetness touched her skin, it brought back all the emotions that had consumed her when she opened the door to the barn on that terrible day and saw Ben. The sweaty panic of it. How everything she knew, felt, hoped for, turned the color of ash.

She watched the rainwater form beadwork on the rolling pin, and she ran her finger through it to shape a noose. When she looked at Ben, his neck was broken at the same dreadful, twisted angle as she remembered. But instead of a lifeless pasty look on his face, his eyes were open, his mouth smiled broadly, and his finger pointed at her.

She narrowed her eyes . . .

Her heart pounding . . . quaking . . .

Her breath chugged in and out of her laboring lungs. She tried to scream. Tried to run. But couldn't. Everything around her was cold, soundless . . .

Her throat burned . . . bile rose . . .

Ben's accusatory finger . . . his eyes frozen open . . . filled with shock . . . smiling . . . smiling . . . She tried to scream again, but then she woke, startled, edgy, confused.

She blinked, became semi-conscious, and sat up, unsure of her surroundings. Her entire body tingling, cold, and clammy. But once she shook herself out of the turbulent haze of the nightmare, and regained her focus, she realized she had fallen asleep on the couch in the living room. She had dreamt of Ben's death before, many times in fact, but they had never been linked with Frankie.

ᔰ ◆ ᔰ

It was almost one in the morning and, as usual, Frankie wasn't home yet. Probably shagging his high school dropout, under-aged girlfriend, Tammy Sue.

"The 7-ll girl," Winter called her.

She had no problem with Frankie hanging out with the guys, but his lurid affairs with his blowsy broads offended her, especially his little convenience store strumpet. When one of

Winter's girlfriends sloughed off Frankie's debauchery by saying, "That's how guys are," it pissed her off even more. So many
of her female friends were so willing to forgive their man for
cheating on them. For some utterly idiotic reason, they believed
men—the poor unfortunate creatures that they were—could
not help being driven by their dangly parts.

Being with Frankie, she was beginning to believe men were
driven by greed, the chase, and lust. Not all, but most. And if
you didn't give it to them when they asked for it, they tried all
the harder to get it. Men, in general, she thought, were simple-
minded varmints that acted like Pavlov's dog if you undid your
blouse to the second button or showed off your navel.

꙳ ◆ ꙳

When Winter found out about the affair with the 7-11 girl,
she drove right over to the Happy Haven trailer park, a few
hundred yards from the 7-11. Tammy lived with her mother,
Bert (short for Roberta), in a faded yellow and brown two-tone
double-wide, scattered among others brimming with uneasy
expectancy, packed tightly together like cows to slaughter.

Bert's uncut front yard, no larger than a postage stamp,
screamed with weeds, and a front door awning sagged to match.
A pale muddy water mark skirted the perimeter of the mobile
home from when White River crested a few years before, flooding Happy Haven. Most everyone in town was surprised and disappointed that the trailers survived after the water receded.

When Winter knocked on the screen door, Bert peered
through the mesh with narrowed eyes, "Y'all still slingin' hash
at Kathy's?" Bert said with a smirk.

Bert was tall and thin but still carried a baby belly. She wore bright red, tight-to-the-skin calf-length pedal pushers and a lime-green blouse—if she stood near an intersection, she'd be a traffic light. She had thick honey-blonde hair, coarse as a broom, pulled up in a loose bun with stray tendrils spiking out in all directions. She was older than Winter by a couple of years, dropping out of high school when she was a sophomore and never going back.

"Tammy, 'round?" Winter asked, lifting one eyebrow.

"What's that girl gone an' done now?" Bert opened the screen door, holding it with her foot. She cradled a Yorkshire Terrier in her left hand, pressing it tightly against her ample bosom and holding a smoldering cigarette in her other hand. The dog looked like a giant undernourished rat, shaking and shivering as if it had just been smacked for dumping a load on the living room rug.

"You need to put a leash on your daughter an' tell her to stay away from Frankie," Winter said.

"Frankie?" Bert flushed as bright as her slacks. "Really? Why that little sneakin', connivin' little . . ."

"Can I speak with her?" Winter interrupted and thought it was odd how flushed Tammy's mother had gotten, but let the thought pass and said again, "Can I speak with Tammy?"

Bert's jaw tightened. More upset than she needed to be. "Nope, the little tart ain't here . . ." Bert continued, taking a puff and blowing out smoke, "Ain't been 'round for a couple of days now. I betcha Frankie ain't the only guy she's flappin' sheets with. I'll tell her you stopped by when I see her . . . I'll tell her real good, I will. She has no manners like you, and I got. I haven't did nothin' but try t' do right by that girl. Sorry for the trouble she done causin' y'all."

There was a look in Bert's eye that rested uncomfortably in between each word of the apology. It all made sense later when she found out that Frankie had been making his rounds with Bert as well.

❧ ◆ ❧

Winter walked into the kitchen for a cold glass of water to calm her nerves, scolding herself over and over: *Why? Why am I so stupid? . . .*

She was exhausted. Thinking about the dream made her shiver. It was so easy to descend back into the eerie silences and remember the sad images of her past and feel sorry for herself for being stuck in such an oppressive relationship. Staying with Frankie battered her, chipped away at her already wounded spirit. Stealing her individuality. Weakening her mind. Dropping her self-esteem to almost zero, and bleeding away the woman she knew she was.

To make matters worse, she was struggling to make the payments on her father's property. Most of the money they received from renting the farm went to satisfy Frankie's whims. Not only was Frankie using her and cheating on her, but he was also getting drunk, and giving Chelsea a horrible example of what a father was supposed to be like. Then again, in a way, maybe Frankie was the *perfect* example of what a father, or a man, shouldn't be like. Winter was trudging through thick, restless stale air that encircled her like an invisible and malignant vapor. She felt dead—dead, alone, and fed up.

She put the glass of water on the kitchen counter. Her head was spinning. The stresses of the relationship with Frankie, Ben, losing the farm, Chelsea, her mother and father, all of it descended upon her at once. Making her nauseous. So much so, it made the amber-colored glow of the streetlamps that filtered through the kitchen window break against the night in brilliant, multicolored ripples. She steadied herself, closed her eyes, and let the queasiness pass until the floor under her was firm and stable. She took another sip of water and went back to the couch to try and sleep again, hoping this time it would be dreamless. No matter how hard she tried to push back her anxiety-ridden thoughts, she knew the sweet, comforting numbness of sleep was going to escape her.

An hour later, she was right. What was still making her squirm were the images she kept revisiting from the dream. Her mind wouldn't stop bombarding her with question after question: *What happened to my self-esteem? What the hell happened to me?*

❧ ◆ ❧

She tried to relax her fluttering mind and let the sweet, friendly penumbra take over.

But like shards of glass, ragged and sharp, the images of the dream cut painful incisions into the back of her mind—slashing closer and closer to her sanity, tearing at the edges, trying to break her.

The dream had punched right through her, and she said to herself: *You cannot have Frankie hamstring you like this. You cannot allow yourself to be a slave to anyone. You cannot let him make you feel like a prisoner. You cannot. You will not!* She tried to calm herself but thinking about her situation continued to run in an endless loop in her mind, and she couldn't break loose of it.

⌖ ◆ ⌖

Even though Winter's parents had been passionate about their church, she had never been entirely comfortable with anything organized, especially religion, and especially after her father died. She didn't remember much from Sunday school as a child. But for some reason, she never forgot the Lord's Prayer and kept it close to her whenever she needed it.

As of late, at night, whenever she couldn't sleep, and especially when she was in a state of extreme stress and worry—like she was at that very moment—she would say the Lord's Prayer to herself. It had been her mantra, of sorts, through all the desperate and troubled times. Something private. Something no one could take away from her. It relaxed her and never failed to coax her to sleep.

She started with slow breaths to center herself, and silently recited the Lord's Prayer. *Our Father who art in heaven . . .* she inhaled again, slowly . . . *hallowed be thy name . . .* It wasn't until she had repeated the prayer a second time that Winter began to relax . . . *Thy kingdom come, Thy will be done . . .* Her thoughts started drifting and her eyelids became heavy. Somewhere in that drift, she heard the real world break through; the muffled sound of a car rolling up to the house and the soft grind of worn brakes. A car door slamming shut.

Her sleepiness vanished. Footfalls sounded on the front

porch. The front door opened. The screen door slammed against the frame. *Thwack!* Her skin became clammy and cold all over again.

She pretended to sleep, praying Frankie would leave her alone, hoping he wasn't too drunk, or too horny. When he was drunk, it was the worst—the stale smell of alcohol, cigarette smoke clinging to his clothes and soaked into his skin. The bittersweet smell of another woman's perfume.

It was time to stop acting like his doormat. Now all she had to do was marshal enough courage. And things would be better. Because they couldn't be worse. But, as had been the trend, when things couldn't possibly get any worse, it did.

❧ ◆ ❧

The economy took its horrendous dive into the abyss, starting first with Black Monday in 1987, and resulting in the collapse of the lumbering savings and loans industry which compromised the well-being of millions of people in America, not only Winter. When she received the phone call from the bank that her payment for the farm was past due by three months, she closed her eyes, shook her head—the entire world pushed out from underneath her like one thick, long exhale.

Frankie had talked her into putting everything into a savings and loan. When it went under, the note to the farm was sold to a bank. Winter took in a breath that sounded more like a sob, and hung up the phone. She had no idea that Frankie hadn't kept up with the payments for the farm. But she knew exactly how the money was squandered and knew it was gone for good.

She had trusted Frankie with everything. Absolutely every-thing. They had no savings to fall back on. No money to pay the note on the farm. All she had were promises, and since banks didn't run on promises, in an instant, her father's property was gone.

The bank took it all.

‿ ✦ ‿

She had been lying to herself and used denial as a tool.

It had worked well for her in the past. It got her through her parents' deaths and Ben's suicide. But she was tired of waking up in the morning feeling helpless, feeling hopeless. There were no words to put up against her heightened sense of futility. She was figuring out that denial couldn't be used as a blindfold to hide the suffering any longer.

She was done with every lie she had ever told herself, *It's okay to be with Frankie. Maybe Frankie could change?* Or the big-gest lie of all: *Everything will be all right if I just hang on a little longer.*

No. No. No! No more lies.

She was done with every lie she allowed herself to believe about Frankie. Winter knew she had herself to blame for her misfortune. It was *she* who had allowed herself to be taken ad-vantage of by her loser boyfriend. It was *she* who had let the tragedies of her past control her future.

But when the farm had been taken from her, gone forever, something inside her sat up, truly awake for the first time since Ben had died. She knew she had to do something, anything, to get back on track. She had been in such a fog since Ben's death, she didn't think she'd ever find anyone, and that, she believed, was how she let Frankie take advantage of her—a rebound born of her worst nightmare. Frankie, well, he'd been one helluva mistake. Enough was enough. What Winter had to do was simple. But leaving someone, even a jackass like Frankie, is never simple.

ᑯ ◆ ᑔ

It was a terribly harsh truth to realize she lived in fear. She was more disappointed, though, with herself, because she'd exposed Chelsea to such an unfriendly environment.

It isn't easy to deal with the truth. And the toughest part about coping with the truth is accepting it in the first place. People walk miles and miles to avoid having to look at, talk about, or actually try confronting what they know will cause them pain. Short-sighted as it is to wear blinders in a relationship, it still amazes me how many of us do exactly that.

She wondered why, and the answer lay before in the hollowness she felt and the budding of the sadness that she long ago buried. It seemed to her that her entire life had been described and dominated by fear, a gripping terror that she was unwilling to name, let alone face. But all the running she'd done from the past had only brought her to now.

She had been a fool about Frankie, and wrong, so very wrong. It was hard for her to admit. But now, echoing within her, she found an indomitable voice floating to the surface, helping her find the resilience to rise above her fears. It was as if the haze finally lifted from the warmth of the sun. The type of sunlight that burns through the dense mist making you narrow your eyes and lower your head and whisper, *I get it.* Then forces you to lift your head up and open your eyes, so you repeat what you said, but this time you scream it out loud from the top of your lungs to make sure that you really *do* get it.

All she wanted was to find her way back to what made sense in her life and to not be afraid anymore. And for most of us, living in fear and inequity is a powerful goad. *This must end*, she thought to herself. *No more Frankie, no more fear.* The truth was not hard to swallow, and she drank it down in one glorious, satisfying gulp. No one was going to rescue her from her dreary existence, except herself.

⁊ ◆ ⁊

It was around suppertime when Winter confronted Frankie. It was a bone-chilling winter night, and snow had started falling an hour before. She was staring out the kitchen window, entranced by the swirling air as it pushed around a thousand tangled knots of flickering snow that danced across the window pane.

Frankie stood next to the fridge, complaining as he always did. Complaining about how lazy she was; about how she didn't do enough to make ends meet, and how he needed extra cash because he was going to meet his "compadres" later for some suds. She was sitting at the kitchen table, not listening to his chatter, letting the confidence inside her build. Her fingernails, clacking one at a time on the kitchen table, unconsciously drummed out her irritation and the veins on her neck pulsed with a sympathetic rhythm.

She turned to look Frankie squarely in the eye, and when her gaze met his, it held, and she stared at him the way people looked at a natural disaster, a flash flood, perhaps, or a torna-do, stunned and surprised—stunned that she'd gotten involved with Frankie to begin with, and surprised with herself for how she'd almost let Frankie destroy the person she knew she was. She rolled her eyes and looked back out the window and won-dered how she had ever been attracted to him with his big nose, pockmarked skin, eyes all bugged out looking like a toad, face blotched, reddish.

The snow was thickening.

Frankie took a long, overly dramatic drag from his cigarette, inhaling deeply and blowing smoke out as he tilted his head back. Part of her wanted to say: *You sloth. You leech. You moron of a man . . . You're a fuckin' idiot.* But if she did that, all the anger, all the pain, all the heartache gnawing at her would come gush-ing out. *And what if it did?* She thought. *Why should that frighten me?* Acting on angry emotions like the ones bearing down on her would never accomplish anything. She knew that. Angry outbursts, she thought, curdled the moment turning it into a sourness that sticks to the skin; it's difficult to wash out and always escalates to a burning pitch, where only ashes remain. And when you walk away from a disastrous argument like that, you don't feel good about yourself. All that you have left are the reflections of unresolved issues, hurt feelings, and painful memories.

You gain nothing.

❧ ✦ ❧

Winter fixed her eyes on Frankie again. She didn't blink. Just glared straight at him, like hardened steel. As if she'd realized for the first time what a cretin he was.

Her fingernails clacked away. Clack. Clack. Clack.

Frankie scrunched his shoulders and shook his head.

"What?" he questioned. The clacking stopped. Silence separated the distance between them, hanging like a frosty curtain. She tilted her head and squinted, and Frankie repeated forcefully, "What, goddamnit!"

"It's over between us, Frankie." Her voice didn't quaver once. She didn't scream it out. She said it evenly and calmly and straight at him, like an arrow when it finds its target.

More silence.

The adamant tone of her voice surprised Frankie—not that he would have known what the word "adamant" meant. He stood there, frozen. The only movement was the muscle in his jaw as he pressed his teeth tightly together. Winter found herself, found her strength. She was not going to be ruled by fear, nor allow herself to feel like a prisoner anymore.

She was pissed. Pissed for her sake and Chelsea's.

She stood up from the kitchen table, broke the silence and leveled her eyes with his and said, "I'm leaving." In less than two seconds, with two sentences—as short as they were—she had established her authority over Frankie.

The thought did cross her mind that he might become physical with her. He had never done it in the past, but then, she had never threatened to leave him, either. If he did strike her, she was prepared to fight back, no matter the result. She was sure that most men, like Frankie, emotionally abused their women by making disparaging comments, lowering their self-esteem to gain control over them, and wore their tattoos like a shield to conceal their weak character.

"Go ahead, leave!" he replied harshly. "What good are ya t' me, anyway? I should've did that—leave your sorry ass a long time ago."

Then he added in a hushed voice, as if he didn't care, and took another puff of his cigarette. "You wanna leave . . . fine, you know the way out." He exhaled smoke, and with an exaggerated gesture pointed an open palm toward the front door and raised his eyebrows.

He believed he was calling her bluff, but when he saw the glazed look of defiance in Winter's eyes and realized she might mean what she said, he was sure he was about to lose his meal ticket. He thought it better to soften his approach and said, "Hey, look,—don't git all bent." Using his sorry-baby-I'm-an-idiot voice, which always worked in the past. He calmed his speech down and continued, "I didn't mean it like that. C'mon, baby—why'ya gotta be like this?" Winter got up to leave.

Frankie jumped in front of her and opened his arms, prodding her for a hug, and added, "You're actin' like'a overflooded parkin' lot at the Golden Corral. Calm yourself down an' c'mon over here an' let's sit an' talk some more. No reason for us t' be fightin' like this—you know what? You don't need t' be fix nothin' for dinner t' night, we'll go out."

She pushed passed Frankie and out of the kitchen, bumping against his left shoulder with just enough force to prove her point ignoring his open arms. She could smell the scent of him; stale beer and cheap perfume.

For a moment, she thought she heard waves crash against a rocky shore, but it wasn't the ocean. It was the cold brisk wind pushing against the windows and the anger inside her, wailing, and racing through her veins. She was going to say something more, but she decided it would be better to let her anger evaporate like ocean foam on a sandy shore.

❧ ✦ ❧

She had planned everything in advance. She'd packed the car with essentials she and Chelsea would need to start a new life. All the other stuff in the house she had no desire for. It had too much of Frankie smeared all over it, slimy and sticky. Frankie took another puff from his cigarette, acting as if he didn't care and watched as Winter put on her coat and walked into the living room.

Chelsea was sitting on the couch, knees tucked up to her chest, looking scared. She bent down and as quiet as a grave said, "Let's put your coat on." She could see pools of tears and fear in Chelsea's eyes and added, her tone a little stronger, "Everything's gonna be alright."

They walked out the front door and into the night. Frankie followed them outside and continued to throw out insult after insult. "You were nothin' when I met ya. You're nothin' now, an' you'll never be nothin'!" Winter walked down the front steps of the house and onto the sidewalk, turned for an instant, and looked back. The snow was thick, and she could barely see Frankie through all the white swirling between them.

The soft white flakes caked her eyelashes. She blinked them away and continued toward the car. The air seemed as cold as any winter air, yet clean, fresh, new. Every step from the house, away from Frankie, took so little effort as if her determination to tell Frankie off and leave him had lessened the gravity around her. She calmly opened the car door and helped Chelsea get into the backseat. While buckling the seatbelt, her fingers shook. "What's going on, Mommy," Chelsea said in a soft, sniffling voice. She kissed her baby girl gently on the forehead and spoke in her ear, "Don't worry. Everything's okay." Winter wiped Chelsea's tears away and added, "Let's go find us a new home." Then she kissed Chelsea on the forehead again.

And they left.

❧ ◆ ❧

Winter and Chelsea drove off, straight into the future and into a new life. But she couldn't keep herself from glancing in the rearview mirror to see Frankie as a snowy ghost holding his beer in one hand, puffing his cigarette with the other, standing out on the porch in the cold night air in his T-shirt, trying to look macho and still in control. But he wasn't in control. Not anymore. She saw Frankie let out a long stream of smoke as he threw his cigarette onto the porch floor, grinding it with his shoe.

Within a few short—terrible, but electrifying—minutes, Winter's life had changed again. It surprised her that all the time she'd carelessly wasted with Frankie could end like a vague and distant dream.

Like it had never happened.

❧ ◆ ❧

Her hands and legs trembled as the adrenaline and the fierce storm inside her gradually wore off.

She blew out a worked-up sigh of relief, refocused her mind, and drove straight to Bloomington, Indiana. A town far enough from Frankie and the perfect place to figure things out, a college town. A place where she could figure out what to do with her new lease on life. And like the stone-cold fighter she'd just become—a knock-out in the final round—she knew exactly what she was going to do.

∾ ◆ ∾

They stayed in a motel—cheap but clean. What mattered was, they were together, with a new future yet to be written. Within two days, she found a safe place to rent—a sweet, tiny, two-bedroom house. By the end of the week, they had moved in, and she had a job as a waitress in a decent local family restaurant, and Chelsea was enrolled in a new school, walking distance from their new home.

Being a waitress was okay for now. She was good at being a waitress. And in a way, it brought back an old comfort; it was reassuring. Gave her solid ground to stand on. A good, fresh start, as it were. She was no longer willing to put herself in a position, ever again, where the atmosphere around her was dark and uncertain. Never again would she live in fear. She wanted to look forward to the future, and she wanted to create a home where she and Chelsea could feel safe again.

She had laid out a strategy for herself that she believed would help restore stability and develop a solid foundation for her and her daughter to create new and positive experiences together. As a kid, she had loved school, excelled in it, and always dreamt of going off to college. Her dad shared the same dream for her. She had applied to two schools and was accepted by both, Indiana University and Purdue University when she was in high school. They had celebrated by going out to dinner at Kathy's Café, and Kathy surprised them with a cake with candles. It was a good memory. When her father died, taking care of the farm superseded her college aspirations. But the desire never wandered far from her thoughts.

❧ ✦ ❧

The following week, Winter had gathered all the information she needed to jump-start her education. There was a two-year college in Bloomington. She would start there. She spoke with an advisor who guided her through the admission requirements, the degree program requirements, and gave her options for financial aid. Her goal was to become a nurse and make health care her profession. She had a friend who was a nurse, who had done the exact same thing. She lived in Bloomington and did very well for herself and her family.

She was a single mother, too.

This inspired her. She knew she could do the same. She was going to make a career for herself. She loved learning, and it would make her feel like she was part of something special—this was an incredible feeling. Knowledge was power, and she knew she was smart enough to do anything she set her mind to. Taking ownership of a good education was by far the best way she knew to start over and rebuild self-worth and self-respect. She also realized what had happened to her, and that what was about to happen from that point on would be something that would show Chelsea that she, too, could do anything once she put her mind to it.

So the seasons folded into each other and life for Winter and Chelsea rolled along in its new cycle of going to work, going to school, and anticipating happier days.

Back At the Lodge With Winter

My coffee was cold. Needed more.

I understood Winter had been paddling through a dense fog and she hadn't been thinking straight after Ben killed himself. That's a no-brainer. And Frankie, well, he wasn't a mystery to me at all. I've dealt with bad relationships before, too, although Frankie was a pretty bad one. Those relationships turn you into a shell of yourself until you have no idea who you are or how to leave.

Unfortunately, Winter didn't see the warning signs.

Often, there aren't any.

Not until the poison has seeped into the veins and heart. And I guess there are times a person needs to get lost to find out who they really are.

You know, find their soul again.

Their crux, as I call it.

Their center.

And frankly, maybe she had to experience a Frankie to figure out all that soul-searching stuff to knock herself out of the fog. The thing is, I felt sorry for her more when she lost the farm than I did about the loser boyfriend. One thing is for sure, losing the farm, well, that had been *really* awful for her. I could tell, for the most part, she had accepted that unfortunate outcome as best she could and had moved on. Moved on rather well, I might add. I also knew it would be something she'd always regret. We can't relive a single moment. We can't unsay things, and we can't undo things. We can only sweep up the pieces of the mess we make and live with the mistakes the best we can.

But I was curious about something else. I was curious about why she worked a full-time job at the diner, worked part-time at the lodge, juggled school while raising her daughter, all that she was doing, as it was right then and there. I knew the answer to my question before I even asked. Still, I asked, "I get it that you needed to be in Bloomington to go back to school. But why the hell are you working at the diner in Bloomington and then driving all this way to work here at the lodge, too—*and* going to school—*and* taking care of Chelsea? I don't see how you can do it all."

She took the last sip of her coffee, smiled at me and jiggled her cup lightly side to side, anticipating my desire for more Java, "I am *woman*," she said and laugh-snorted, put her hand over her mouth surprised she'd snorted, and laugh-snorted again—which I found adorable, by the way. Then she told me, "I need the extra cash. Workin' at the diner isn't enough." She paused as if reflecting and added, "An'—I guess 'cause I grew up here. It's good to be 'round people you know an' trust. It grounds you. You know what I mean?"

I did know what she meant.

Even I understood the importance of being around people that could be trusted. It had been years since I'd stayed in one place long enough to where I could develop, long-lasting friend-ships. So I knew exactly how Winter felt.

That was part of her crux I admired so much.

I stood up and took her cup. She looked up at me and said, "Thanks. I could use a pick-me-up."

I replied, "You're doing the right thing, Winter. I admire that."

As I walked to the kitchen to get our refills, many thoughts raced through my mind about Winter and how brave she had been to put the most significant things in her life back into order. Her life may not have been what she'd set out for in the beginning. It certainly wasn't how she may have planned it. And it may seem cruel that fate had thrown Ben and then Frankie into her path, but fate has its own agenda and its own reason for teaching us life's lessons. That is, if you believe fate has any influence on a person's life. If it does, once it decides what it's going to do, there is no stopping it.

What is important is to be willing and open-minded to the teachings that Providence places in front of us and learn from those lessons.

When I returned, I took a moment to steal a glance at Win-ter through the dining room window before I stepped outside. She looked so small and frail, yet so lovely from the fire's flick-ering glow. It amazed me how she had coped with such adver-sity. I could feel her struggle. It would be difficult for anyone to recover from the tragedies that had been placed upon her lap.

I appreciated our friendship the most at that moment, and I knew the image of Winter sitting by the fire would be with me, burned into my memory. I walked outside and handed her cup of coffee back to her. I put another log on the fire and watched the new flames spit and dance. This somehow brightened my spirit, eased the tension from her story, and made me feel less restless.

I sat down, and she continued . . .

Winter: Reborn

For a long time, after Winter's father and Ben had died, she didn't care all that much about finding happiness again. What had become important was some type of normality, a simple dependability. She had that with Ben for a short time, but he took that away from her, and now she wanted it back. Being with Frankie . . . well, that was just a stupid mistake. No way to explain that one. Except to say, maybe living with Frankie had never really been a permanent destination for Winter. Maybe she didn't know then, but the months she thought she had wasted on Frankie wasn't wasted time but had been merely a window seat without a view, a stopover on the way to a better place, a better life. And perhaps—if fate had anything to do with it—the next stop would be a softer and safer window seat with a much better view.

But now, she felt reborn. She had taken charge of her surroundings and was ready to find happiness again and not chase blindly after it in the hope that it would miraculously appear. Nothing really mattered except to take each day as it presented itself, good or bad, work hard, and look after her daughter. She would never get her family farm back. As painful as that was, she had accepted that reality, which was—most, decidedly so—a tremendous step forward for her.

ૐ ✦ ૐ

A strange thing it is, the way some of us realize who we are only through misfortune and change—like Winter—reborn from the ashes of lightning strikes that knocked her to her knees.

At that point in her life—finding a new home, going to school, starting fresh and new—it was like she had unlocked a twelve-inch-thick, airtight, steel door, and let the troubles of the old days escape and drift away.

She wasn't naïve. She knew the ghosts of her past misfortunes always floated around her and could, one day—if the chance presented itself, or when she let her guard down—try to cast their spell over her yet again. If and when that happened, she would deal with it the best way she could.

Winter no longer had that terrifying feeling of being wholly and utterly lost. From all the twisting, turning anxiety and disappointments, through all that fertile turbulent soil, the person she used to be broke through—strong, decisive, empowered.

She promised herself, and Chelsea: never again would she

allow them to *ever* be in another situation like the one they'd experienced with Frankie. Absolutely, positively no more toads in their life—not ever.

And with that, Winter made one more promise to herself and said it out loud, "Absolutely, <u>no</u> more men!"

Then she told me about Patrick.

Some things can't be changed
Thunderstorms for instance
The time of our own death
Or the sorrow that follows us when
tragedy is determined to walk in our shoes
However
some things can be changed
All that's needed is to be brave enough
to walk in a different direction . . .

Excerpts from the author's journal, On The Road.

— Wednesday, June 22, 1983

Arrived in Muscatine, Iowa, late at night and
watched an old abandoned warehouse burn to the ground.
Amazing feeling watching flames leap thirty feet in the air.
The guy next to me was smoking.
I don't smoke but bummed one off of him anyway.
Don't know why, just had to have a smoke.

•   •   •

— Saturday, September 03, 1983

A few months later — I'm still in Muscatine.
I met an eighty-four-year-old man and have been
working for his landscaping company for the past year.
This old dude is a hoot!
A real ladies man when he was young.
And what a swinger still.
One day I will write a story about his life.

Intermission

Painful Experiences

*L*et's take a short break so I can personally say a couple of things to you. If you like, take a moment. I can wait. . .

I know it's evident that Winter and Patrick will meet, and they do. It is sad that I feel the need to condense all the beautiful moments they had together when they first met, but I know if I didn't, this story would have legs that would never stop growing.

Most of the events that occur in our lives, mainly the day-to-day happenings, are only interesting to those who experience them. In reality, the average person has maybe a couple profoundly significant moments in his or her life that would be interesting enough for someone to write about.

Despite this story's compactness, I am confident you will conclude straightaway, Patrick is a good match for Winter and vice versa, and I am sure you will agree their meeting was a genuine case of synchronicity if there ever was one.

I am acutely aware that so far in this story I've been extremely redundant in hammering home the burdensome, and sometimes punishing, and painful experiences that Winter had in dealing with the shadows of her past. I am sure you were worn out by it.

I must tell you up front: I'm not done with the hammering. I call it the pesky little redundancies of life, which shackle us. Hold us down. Uncomfortable to read about, and even more challenging to overcome. Don't we all replay our most painful experiences over and over again in our minds, creating different scenarios, desperately trying to make sense of it all, and wishing things could have been different?

Absolutely we do, provided we have a conscience.

There are always echoes, always dark and turbulent phantoms sequestered somewhere in everyone's past that pepper us with pain and define our sunny days. Memories can resurface. Wounds can reopen. The roads some of us walk will have demons beneath.

Perhaps suffering is the universal experience of all humans?

∽

I have a couple of unpleasant shadows that are irritatingly redundant and still come to me in unguarded moments.

And while sitting here at my desk scribbling this tale, it has jarred loose those hurtful experiences I war against. They hover in the back of my mind as foggy, out-of-focus ghosts, and invade my thoughts—uninvited—from time to time and are loose threads, untidy parts I'd like to change. When they do float into the light and refocus, I painfully relive the experiences all over again.

For example, once, while I was living in Hawaii, I was leaving the covered parking garage at the Ala Moana shopping center. A rusted, beat-up, barely running, brown and white van cut me off at the exit ramp. I honked my horn and yelled out, "What the hell, dude?" The next thing I knew some large two hundred and fifty–pound, pumped-up, local Samoan—looking like he lived at the gym—wearing a T-shirt that read "Ke ea Hawai'i" (Hawaiian Sovereignty Movement), jumped out of his van, strutted over to my open window, crumpled his forehead, and yelled, "Eh! Bra! Why you honk da kine?"◆ (Translation: "Hey! Asshole! Why you honk your horn?") Without breaking his stride, he coldcocked me on the left side of my face, and added, "Go back t' da Mainland, fuckin' haole!"✶ I was lucky because I turned my head away at the moment his fist was about to crash into my cheek. If I hadn't, he would have shattered my eye socket.

Fortunately, his fist glanced off my face leaving me minor bruising and one hell of a headache later, but didn't knock me out. Knocked me over on my side, though. Still, he wasn't finished with me yet.

He tried forcing his big girth through my open window, reaching for my car keys but because of his monstrous size, he couldn't get all the way in. No matter, I grabbed the keys before he could. That pissed him off more. So he decided to pound more shit out of me (I'm being figurative), repeating over and over with each whomp, "Fuckin' haole! (whomp, whomp), Fuckin' haole! Fuckin' haole!"

When he was finished using me as his personal haole

◆*da kine: A word used in Hawaii when one cannot immediately remember a word.*
✶*haole: A word used mainly in Hawaii to describe a white person. Depending on how you say it, the word can mean either an insult or just a fact.*

punching bag, he walked back to his van, stopped halfway, flipped me off, and then drove part way out of parking garage. His brake lights brightened. The van stopped. The driver-side door opened. I thought, *shit, what now?* Without hurrying, he walked back to my car and stood next to the car door. He paused and stared at me, then bent forward (his face inches from my face) resting his large stubby hands on the open window ledge and said in a soft husky voice, "We understand each other. Right, brah." It wasn't a question.

I had a fleeting thought when he sashayed back to his van, of running him over and breaking some bones. But didn't. Mainly because it would be my luck I wouldn't kill him, and I'd spend ten to twenty years in a cell next to him at the Halawa Correctional Facility (a nice way of saying penitentiary), waiting for a shank to be thrust into my back.

At night—not often, but sometimes—in the moments before I doze off, when the correlation between life and sleep are in flux, I can see that beat-up, old, rusty van and the Samoan with his clenched fist at the edge of my dream, racing toward me.

It amazes me how many times that frightening moment jumps into my head. It's an uneasy, anxiety-ridden memory, to say the least, and each time it comes forward, I wished I had done this, or that, something different than what I did. So, I understand how Winter felt and how difficult it was for her to let go of her demons.

⊸

The incident changed me, of course, and put an unfortunate hole in my life—a gap that increases in size each time the memory rises to the surface. Soon after I had the living daylights beaten out of me, I left Hawaii and paradise far behind.

Don't get me wrong; the people of Hawaii are intelligent, loving, and kindhearted people. They are descendants of a long line of courageous voyagers and fearless warriors. Their word 'ohana', which means "family", is not strictly a word, it is the cornerstone of their humanity and benevolence, whether you're blood-related, adopted, or haole. I do not blame the Hawaiian people for one individual who used the race card as an excuse for his own failures in life.

No matter where one lives, there will always be a few rotten apples in an orchard, even in paradise.

⌇

I would like to think that there is a purpose to everything Winter went through, and what all of us must go through. Part of that purpose is to test us, and to impart a tiny bit of wisdom we can use, and to show us what is important, and to make us better people.

Yes, I would like to think that.

Okay, enough about me . . . Back to Winter.

At least once in our lives
we will all be touched by adversity
But at some point
we must refuse to be held by it . . .

Excerpt from the author's journal, On The Road.

– Saturday, November 22, 1986

Been living in Provo, Utah.
Staying at the Provo Hotel, downtown Provo, for the past six
months.
Walking among the Mormons.
Remarkable history here.
I've been performing pantomime in elementary
schools and meeting fascinating people with interesting lives.
Got a part playing a postman in a children's TV show at the
Donny and Marie Osmond production center.
Will stay a while longer . . .

Part Three

CHAPTER IV

Patrick

Friday, February 02
Early Morning: Sunrise.
Groundhog Day. Cloudy.
A good day to write and take a long nap . . .

Patrick *lived down* south in Louisville, Kentucky. I never met the man, but in a way, I did get to know him through Winter. When she told me about Patrick, her country-girl cadence changed, softened. It became affectionate, like a slow dance, accessible and thoughtful. From her description, if Patrick and I had actually met, I believe we would have become good friends.

No doubt about it.

But I suspect a little jealousy would have also been rooting around in the back of my thoughts since he had captured Winter's eye and I hadn't.

I do believe, though, at this point Winter had found solid ground, and her feelings for this man weren't coming from anywhere but an honest, wide-eyed, and awakened heart. I am confident she wasn't about to do a Frankie repeat.

And yes, if it isn't shamelessly apparent, Patrick is the guy, the real would-be prince in this story.

A Warning About This Chapter

The fact that I was never introduced to Patrick to know his side of
Winter's story means I had to be inventive and weave my words
between the lines—more from Patrick's point of view
and not as much as from mine.
Some of which is conjecture for sure,
but most of which was from Winter.
Knowing this, you might conclude and say to me,
"Thomas, your story will lack credibility."
I would reply,
"That may be true . . . and yet, here we are just the same,
standing together with nowhere else to go but forward."

Patrick's Story

Winter's Patrick had a strong foothold in one of the
most prestigious law firms in Louisville. A great job
with great promise. He couldn't have asked for anything more
when it came to what he wanted out of life. Or so he thought.

Patrick hadn't planned time away from the office, but the
unexpected happened in the best possible sense, the most
rewarding and serendipitous of events that can befall an up-

wardly mobile young lawyer. He had been handed a high-profile case, and the partners of the firm had promised him if he clinched it, he'd receive a promotion, the next step to becoming a partner. If that happened, he would become the youngest junior partner in the long-standing history of the firm.

The lawsuit had all the earmarks of being vexatious, but Patrick was sure he could have it all wrapped up and handed back to the partners before the firm's annual Halloween party at the end of October.

❧ ◆ ❧

The firm gave him boxes and boxes of files to look over, and six weeks off from his regular duties so he could devote one hundred percent of his attention to the particulars of the case.

Immerse himself in the files.

Get acquainted with his client.

Make sure his defense was perfect in every detail.

Don't eat, sleep, or shave for days.

But none of that bothered Patrick in the least. He was made for hard work and long hours. He was ready, eager, and able to deliver precisely what he knew the partners of the firm expected from him.

Every up-and-coming lawyer dreams of a trial like the one he'd been handed. It was a once-in-a-lifetime judicial proceeding. It could make his reputation, and if he won, he could write his own ticket, so to speak. Later, if he decided that working for a large firm and being a partner wasn't what he wanted, he could start a small practice of his own.

Yes, he believed he, more than the other newbies at the

firm, deserved to be a partner. Not because he was the hardest worker at the firm, although he was, but because he had worked his ever-loving buns off his entire life. From his first job, when he'd turned ten years old, as a gas station attendant at a Shell station (which ironically was one block from his office building), to busing tables all through law school. He thought about starting a small practice in a small town. It was always hiding in the back of his mind. He'd be equally satisfied to deal with the everyday Joe off the street and to help them with their needs, like wills, and deeds and what attorneys in his firm labeled two-bit contract disputes. Nothing wrong with that, he thought.

What was essential to Patrick was being proud of the work he did. No better way to feel good about yourself than helping people with their basic needs. It didn't matter to him in the least if he worked for a large upscale firm or if he had a tiny one-stop-do-it-all lawyer's office of his own.

Yet the dream he'd had when he was in law school, of being a great lawyer, was now tempered by watching the senior partners he worked for. He thought they were highly principled men, incorruptible, but they had an arrogance about them that played thicker at the ends than what Patrick thought an attorney really needed. Plus it seemed to Patrick as if they had reached a pinnacle with their careers and didn't care all that much about the little guy anymore. They focused all their energy on the big corporations and big money. Patrick didn't want to end up that way and promised himself he wouldn't. Nothing like having options, though. Either way, small-town practice or big-city firm, he knew he'd be happy.

Most folks thought Patrick was handsome in an effortless

way—stylish, but never flashy; dashing yet always a gentleman; bright but never flauntingly so; aggressive and judiciously efficient, especially in the courtroom. Confidence clung to him like a tailor-made three-piece suit. He immediately gained respect for his dutiful work habits, and everyone at the firm found him a trustworthy and highly competent attorney. He was proud of his accomplishments, but not too proud. Staying humble had always been his credo. At the time, Patrick felt exceedingly good about his career and thoroughly enjoyed working with everyone at the law firm.

෯ ◆ ๛

It was almost the end of spring. When the partners of the firm gave Patrick his six-week relief from day-to-day duties, he liked the idea of easing up on his usual grunt work and especially liked the change from his daily routine. Six weeks was plenty of time to figure out all he needed to know about the case. Actually, more time than was necessary with a trial scheduled for the end of August.

It was the middle of the workday. Noon, to be exact. On a Friday. Patrick was just finishing his lunch, a ham sandwich on rye, and a half-pound of macaroni salad that he'd picked up at the corner butcher shop and deli. Something he did almost every day. Some days he would eat at the deli, sitting in the back and watching all the lunchtime activity instead of taking his food back to his office. He enjoyed the atmosphere, people talking, butchers calling orders back and forth.

The owners and workers all knew him and called him Lawman. "Hey Lawman. Bologna or ham today?"

"C'mon, Pete . . . it's Friday . . . I always have ham on Friday, with the works—extra everything."

In a renovated, hundred-year-old, twelve-story brick and limestone warehouse, Patrick's office occupied one corner on the tenth floor. It was a medium-sized room, had the original oak hardwood flooring along with bookshelves, stuffed with law books that filled the length of one entire wall. Next to the bookcase were two diamond-patterned, upholstered wingback chairs for clients that faced his work desk. A conference table with six chairs sat to the left.

Standing behind his desk, Patrick stepped up to the buff-curtained window and gazed out over the city landscape taking a bite of his sandwich. He could see his old stomping grounds and the Shell gas station, catty-corner from the deli, looking exactly as it had when he worked there as a kid. The steeple of the old Holy Trinity Parochial School towered above the old brick buildings and majestically looked down on the rooftops, five blocks to the west. Patrick smiled and thought about how he had roamed all through the alleys in that neighborhood, dumpster diving for treasure and playing street hockey with his buddies. He could still hear the thwack and feel the vibration of his hockey stick connecting with the puck, the laughter and excited screams when someone made a goal.

⤳ ◆ ⤨

Growing up in Louisville hadn't been easy for him, but there were moments during his childhood, like hockey games and running with the neighborhood scalawags, that filled days with refuge and helped him forget about his privations.

He placed the empty container of macaroni salad and the sandwich wrapping into the takeout bag and dropped it into the small trash next to his chair. He sat down, put his elbows on his desk, his chin between his fists, and looked at the framed flowered dress hanging on the wall. He swiveled his chair around to gaze out the window again, and that's when he thought, why not take a couple weeks off from work. Take a short working vacation. He hadn't had a vacation in almost three years, maybe a couple of long weekends, but that had been it. *Nothing like a quiet drive up north to Indiana to visit friends*, he thought. *I can work on the case. Get out and into the woods. Do some hiking. Breathe some fresh country air. Clear my mind.*

His paralegal and his secretary, Thelma, could reach him if anything pressing came up. Plus, he'd be no more than two and a half hours away and could return in a heartbeat if there were an emergency. Patrick stepped up to Thelma's desk and handed her a legal pad with notes on it. "Thelma, I'm driving up to Bloomington, Indiana, tomorrow."

"I had a feeling you might," Thelma responded, placing the notepad on her desk. "I've got everything under control." She stood up and handed Patrick his suit coat.

"You always surprise me." Patrick put his coat on and started to leave.

"How long will you be away?"

"Not sure—at least a week. Maybe two," Patrick replied over his shoulder. "If anything comes up I can be back in no time."

"You'll need these," Thelma said, patting two large file boxes and grinning. Patrick stopped, turned, and smiled back.

"Oh, right."

"I've got everything organized—well, for the most part. You can do the rest," she said with a smile. "And don't work every day. Do something fun—go out . . . I don't know, maybe meet someone? Go on a date? Have a real life."

❧ ◆ ❧

Patrick never needed an alarm clock, no matter how early he had to get up. He would always wake before the alarm went off.

It was six in the morning. He sat up, didn't hesitate, threw the bedcovers off, jumped out of bed, and showered. Twenty minutes later he sprinted out of his apartment carrying his well-used military-green duffel bag over his shoulder and holding a red mini cooler in his hand. He vaulted into his car, anxious to get started on his vacation. He then placed the cooler in just the right position on the passenger's seat for easy access; it held a couple of cold cokes, a bag of nuts, and two candy bars, for quick snacks on the road.

In the middle of the night, the heavens had opened, cleft by immense flashes of lightning that momentarily lifted the veil of darkness, and thunder that shook the air, pouring out spring rain in steady sheets. Now, scattered, pale storm clouds remained, dissolving into a faded smoky white, pushed by the breeze, as the thunder ceased, leaving everything washed and rejuvenated.

A few weeks before, he had purchased a new car. One should say, it was new to him. He wouldn't allow himself a fancy, look-at-me-I'm-a-lawyer, brand spanking new car right off the showroom floor. He didn't like the attention or need anything extravagant. All he needed was something nice enough that clients would respect him—and suitably reliable to ferry him to and from work each day.

❧ ◆ ❧

During high school, Patrick had fallen in love with muscle cars. He liked their simplicity and loved their racy edginess. He knew a hopped-up, dead to rights motor-monster would always be in demand, but that wasn't his style. While some of his buddies were big motor-head show-offs, turning their driving machines into muscle cars on steroids and roasting tires on Friday nights, Patrick would cruise around town, nice and comfortable, in his 1966 Mustang. One day, he thought, his Mustang would be a classic. He tried hanging out with the dragsters a couple of times, but a night with that bunch always ended in some brawl or with the police breaking up the scene and arresting someone. Plus, they smoked weed and were drunk most of the time.

Patrick wasn't into that.

As far as Patrick was concerned, nothing seemed more satisfying than cruising in his Tahoe Turquoise Mustang, taking a date to the A&W Root Beer stand for cheeseburgers and onion rings, then heading off to Becker's Motor Drive-in for a late-night movie and necking in the back seat. He always thought it crazy to waste a night drag racing when you could enjoy an evening with a sweet Southern belle.

❧ ◆ ❧

Patrick had driven his '66 Mustang, a straight, simple, standard six-cylinder coupe all through college. The only thing flashy about it was its turn signals. His sweet, sexy '66 had been his most prized possession. It had been the first big purchase of his life, and on top of that, his first car, and like everything else he owned, he had kept his Mustang in remarkably good shape.

He'd made a lot of great memories with that car. Plus, he felt and looked so damn cool driving it. He was okay with looking cool, but the chance for an actual partnership in the law firm superseded his love for driving his classic car. Being cool he thought, was better suited for real cool guys like James Dean, Steve McQueen or Marlin Brando—when he was younger—not a young lawyer. Plus, having two cars just wasn't practical. And Unfortunately, a 1966 Mustang didn't make the grade in the "looking responsible" department.

He promised himself when the time was right, and after he was a partner at the firm, he would own another muscle car. This time, it would be for the sheer pleasure of driving a classic, and of course, looking cool. He suspected his practicality came from being bounced from one foster family to another as a kid, never knowing when he'd be shuffled off to the next foster home in the middle of the night. Those experiences were the reasons he'd limit himself to just enough personal items that could be stuffed into the only piece of luggage he owned—his military-green duffel bag.

Patrick took care of everything he owned or had, including every stitch of clothing. If one of his casual weekend shirts started to fray or unravel along the edges, he'd get out his needle and thread and fix it. Buying something new was a luxury Patrick didn't have as a kid. Even now, when he could afford virtually any automobile he desired, he spent his money with sober regard for what it took to earn it. So he purchased a pre-owned car instead of a new one. It was nice enough, clean enough, and lawyer-looking enough.

After selling the Mustang so he could purchase the new/used car, he made a profit on the deal. His practicality unquestionably proved its worth. There was only one problem with his new ride. His chances of looking cool were out of the question.

❧ ◆ ❧

Patrick slipped behind the wheel of his not-so-fancy 1988 twilight blue (uncool, lawyer-looking) Thunderbird, opened a candy bar, started the engine, and took off to visit friends in Bloomington. As he drove, listening to the powerful rumble of the Thunderbird's well-built V8, he watched the countryside zip past, and drifted to comforting thoughts of visiting his friends and the exciting prospect of where his life was headed. When anyone asked him what he hoped his life would be like one day, he'd always reply, *I don't know? It's a mystery—but I can't wait to find out.*

The friends he planned his two-week vacation around weren't merely friends, they were the family he never had. He was a POTS project, a "Product of The State," as he always described himself. An orphan spinning aimlessly through the system, who'd been left on the doorstep of one of Louisville's orphanages, wrapped in a woman's tattered, flowery cotton dress—born only hours before. Patrick had no idea who his parents were, or even if they were alive. When he was old enough, he was raised at, Holy Trinity, a parochial school that boarded orphans and runaways.

His line of descent began the moment one of the brothers at the orphanage picked him up from the doorstep, took him inside, wrote a report about the incident, and put it in a file folder. A greenish-gray recycled paper folder with a name written on it—a name not of his choosing and sitting in one of many dusty, tan-colored steel file cabinets that were lined up along the walls in the basement, like tin soldiers in a show of ranks, saluting their captain. When Patrick became a lawyer, he petitioned the state to allow him access to his file, which they granted. Not only did he receive the records, but he was also given the well-worn flowered dress he'd been found in—he believed to be his mother's dress—which he displayed in a shadow box that hung on the wall facing his work desk in his office. A framed reminder of his past.

☙ ◆ ❧

He struggled in school but worked harder than most to make good grades, knowing that education was his true salvation. Being a high achiever in school gave Patrick the sense of accomplishment that he hungered for, and he had also been one heck of an athlete.

He excelled in all sports—wrestling, swimming—but he was made for football. Patrick's athletic prowess earned him a full scholarship to Indiana University. He used that scholarship to his advantage because he had no aspirations whatsoever to bang heads as a football player for the rest of his life. As an IU student, he took charge of his study groups, always choosing school over parties.

He worked nights in a bar, busing tables, and saved as much as he could before he graduated. Those who watched him play football said he ran like the wind. That's what he believed he'd been doing all his life; running like the wind. When people asked him how he could play football so well and still maintain top grades in school, he'd tell them, as he held up a tennis ball: *This is my inspiration. When I look at this tennis ball, it reminds me of how a dog's eyes are fixed on it with absolute conviction. Move the ball to the right, and the dog follows the ball. Move it to the left, and the dog follows it. Up, down, the dog's eyes never lose sight of the ball.*

That is precisely how Patrick treated *everything* he did, never taking his eyes off the ball. He seemed to have it all worked out. There was no question he had a great job, a plan for the future, and a 1988 Ford Thunderbird—which was *not* part of his plan. But he was always prepared for the unexpected.

In a way, it was that awareness of the unexpected that kept him from finding trouble before trouble found him.

❧ ◆ ❧

While at college, Patrick and his roommate, Dan, instantly became best friends, inseparable. And Dan's parents, Bill and Maureen, had adopted Patrick into their family as if he were their own.

He and Dan shared a rare bond; they were more like brothers than friends (I'm not going to go into detail, but if it weren't for Patrick, Dan most likely wouldn't have graduated), and Dan's parents were the only people Patrick felt comfortable enough with to deputize as his surrogate mother and father. For Patrick, there was no better place in the world to spend his off time than with his adopted parents and his best friend, Dan.

꙰ ◆ ꙰

The drive up to Bloomington was something he'd always enjoyed, especially motoring along the back roads. He could think
of no better way to enjoy the countryside.

Making that trip always put him in a good mood, especially
during the spring when the dogwood and redbud trees found
their voices and scattered their songs along the roadside with
such vibrant shades of pink and white. Each spring he was never disappointed in how vivid the flowers of the redbud trees
could shine and how the lace-like dogwood flowers made the
trees appear as if they were laden with snow.

Moments like that were so beautiful and privately his. They
always brought a sense of surprise—a surprise that mingled
with admiration for something so simple as a dogwood flower,
and that a flower could bring such peace to his frame of mind.
The unpredictable nature of the world around him was a part
of life Patrick held in high regard, always embracing the unan-
ticipated because good things could happen if you opened your
heart to the unknown.

Patrick had never married; he never wanted to, fearing it
might distract him from his goals. Life was good. However, a
steady income could put a man in a particular frame of mind.
This was one of those times for Patrick. For the most part, he
believed his life was exactly where it needed to be, and he was
happy—happy and content in the way most single men are.

Although, floating around lightly in the back of his reasoning, and growing stronger day by day, was the mounting avid-

ity to find a special someone. Someone with whom he could share the good times and the bad. Someone he could adore, and someone who would adore him; someone to build a home with, make a family with, and trust to be by his side to the absolute end. That had been on his mind a lot.

As for children, he would let that work itself out. He wasn't willing to completely plot out his life like writers do a good novel. He loved the mystery and the magic that each day offered. He thought it was always good to make plans, but at times, he believed, he had to let what happened happen and make each moment count for something. One thing he knew for sure, he'd be an excellent father. Since he hadn't had a father of his own when growing up, he was committed to one day having the chance to be a good father. When he thought of what his family would be like, he always liked the idea of having a girl. *Yes, a daughter would be nice*, he thought.

The fact was, Patrick knew he was the perfect candidate for husbandry and fatherhood. He believed, more than anything, there was nothing more important a man, or woman, could do with his or her life, than have a family.

❧ ◆ ❧

When Patrick arrived in Bloomington and rode up the driveway of his adopted parents' home, he knew he'd made the right decision to spend time away from the office. It felt so good to be home, to be with family. He didn't realize how much he missed seeing them until everyone hugged each other. Bill and Maureen looked strong and healthy, but it was easy to tell that age was strolling alongside them.

The reunion spilled over with joyous laughter; there was steak for dinner—cooked on the grill with all the trimmings—and storytelling late into the evening. Nothing could have been more enjoyable. Patrick decided he should do such things more often and promised himself he would.

∾ ◆ ∾

The next day, they all went downtown to the square to shop around and have lunch. Whether you believe in fate or not, I am sure you won't be surprised when I tell you that Patrick's adopted parents took him to the very same restaurant where Winter worked. As destiny plays with our minds and pushes us from here to there and back again, it gave Patrick and Winter a gentle nudge toward each other. The very moment Patrick walked into the diner, he noticed Winter.

Over the course of his lunch, an enjoyable numbness gently coated his thoughts, and his emotions became tangled and twisted. That's my flowery way of stating the obvious. Most men instantly lose their peripheral vision when they see a pretty face. And with Winter, every man who looked into her eyes was a little blinded in one way or the other.

Patrick had always found pretty women easy to find—mostly, though, they found him. Although such physical attributes were nice in a female, he was hoping that hidden under Winter's attractive looks was something more profound, something wonderfully passionate, something unique.

Her kindheartedness was obvious. It was written in the way she smiled and talked to customers. He found it adorable how she casually helped herself to a peek in his direction when she jotted down someone's order, or when she was clearing and cleaning tables. What surprised him the most, though, was that each time she brushed by him, without realizing it, he found himself grinning.

He knew she was going to be trouble.

Trouble in the right way.

❧ ◆ ❧

Winter had been aware of Patrick as well, but she was far more removed, hiding her emotions in long deep-set trenches. And yet, she found herself smiling, too, each time she walked past Patrick's table or asked whether he was enjoying his meal.

This caught her off guard.

Patrick was a good-looking man in a conventional sense— one would suppose—but not extraordinarily so, she thought. His looks didn't matter to her. But she found it difficult not to sneak glances at him, and wonder what sort of man he might be.

That day, Patrick carried a shadow of a beard on his face, which lent him an outdoorsy ruggedness, an honest, hard-wor-kin' Hoosier farmer charm, if you will. Shave the twelve o'clock shadow, and he'd have that all-American clean-cut look. One might say, a tall drink of charged water. The type of guy who could split wood all day long without breaking a sweat, utterly comfortable in his own skin, with a controlled understated con-fidence. Nothing about Patrick was forced or manufactured. He was definitely not the typical man who prowled around in Winter's neck of the woods.

His light brown hair was well trimmed but still looked

natural, as if he had just pushed it into place with his hands. He had a narrow face, with a small wisp of hair falling over his forehead that set off his striking baby-blue eyes that were hypnotic and seductive. The kind of eyes a woman could gaze into for hours and question if they were real; she saw understanding in those eyes as they studied her, making something jump inside her, an unexpected interest to find out what type of man Patrick was.

ᔔ ◆ ᔕ

There was something openly uncommon about Patrick, or maybe a better description would be, there was something unquestionably notable about him.

Up close, when she served his food, he smelled both familiar and exotic, like fresh cut hay in early summer. There were times, though, when something would ignite a memory and rip open her wounds. Perhaps the scent of a flower, or a song on the radio, or a love scene in a movie. Nothing about Patrick triggered any memory of the pain of the lightning strikes she carried with her. That was a good sign.

Then she remembered. She had solemnly vowed, *No more men*—actually, her exact words had been: *Absolutely, no more men.* I think Winter thought she meant it when she said no more men. But that promise could never stop the attraction she was feeling toward Patrick—yet, with equal measure, she was fearful of opening a gateway to her heart wide enough to allow another someone in. *Once a doorway is open to love again,* she thought, *things could break.* Yes, she knew it was a chance everyone takes.

But concealed within the hollow space, where she kept secrets hidden from everyone, she desperately longed to open the floodgates and let love rush over her, and give her a chance to spend a lifetime with someone exceptional—someone who would have the very same understanding and enthusiasm about love that she had.

She told herself, *Two things could happen if I reach out. I could have my heart stomped on again, or he could be my one and only.* Then she thought, maybe a third thing could happen, *We'd just become splendid friends.* She shook her head to shake out all those crazy thoughts and laughed at herself for having such cravings about a man she hadn't even officially met yet, or might not meet. Once again she remembered the promise she made to herself about men.

༂ ♦ ༂

Watching Winter, Patrick immediately became aware of the clumsiness he always suffered around women he found even remotely appealing. *You're a flippin' lawyer, for Pete's sake,* he said to himself. *Stop acting like a pansy.*

Patrick's friends were herding themselves out of the restaurant and were beckoning Patrick to hurry it up. On the way out while Patrick was still sitting at the table, Dan leaned close to his ear and said, "If you don't ask that girl out you've been eyein' all during lunch, I will."

Patrick scooted the chair back from the table as he watched his buddy leave. Dan turned and looked straight at Patrick as he went out the door pointing to Winter with a smile and mouthing, "She's mine." The lawyer voice inside Patrick took control, and he couldn't help himself, regardless of how awkwardly he'd been acting. Only women he could tell were unique frightened him. Winter frightened him, but in the right way.

Patrick stood up, keeping his eyes sharp on Winter, and ventured over to the cash register where she was finishing up with a customer. He walked with a relaxed manner, not overly confident, but in a way that troubled her because it made her feel good—really good.

"I was just thinking," Patrick started to say when he handed her his credit card to pay the bill, "—well, not just thinking, but kinda thinking . . . I mean," Patrick faltered. His mind, his senses, all his synapses were sputtering.

That's crazy, he thought.

He tried to relax, compose, but his words still came out tangled, "—if you had any free . . . extra . . . free time I mean, maybe we could have dinner together?" *Great! That was smooth,* he thought to himself.

Winter took his MasterCard, glanced at him in a somewhat protective way. She thought, *"How cute. The man doth fluster."* Then she squinted one eye in a suspicious but flirting way, and replied, "I don't think so," She turned away from him, punched the numbers on the cash register, and went on, "Sorry. Don't know you."

"How about dinner tonight?"

Winter smiled, maybe more dubious than inviting and handed his MasterCard back to him, with a pen and the receipt and said curtly, "Sign here." Right away she blasted herself with thoughts like: *Why did I just shut him down? I know why . . . I'm being careful . . . No . . . I'm being stupid . . . Just say yes, idiot . . . Oh my god, look at his blue eyes.* Then, for some inexplicable reason, her mind went completely blank.

There was a tiny bell hooked to a spring above the screen door of the restaurant so that each time the door opened the bell would ring. The bell made its pint-sized ping as a customer walked through the door and she thought about the movie, *It's A Wonderful Life*, when the little girl Zuzu said, "Every time a bell rings, an angel gets their wings." She wondered if it was different for a restaurant and every time a bell would ring, maybe a gal would get her guy? Doubtful. It was a silly thought, which made her smile.

"Well, then," Patrick said undaunted, signing the receipt and handing it back to Winter, gaining control over his earlier lack of coordination—and his stammering. Without missing a beat this time, he added, "I'm just going to have to have lunch here every day until you do know me." He smiled back. Not dubious in any way, but altogether inviting in every way, making the bell ring again as he opened the screen door and stepped out.

She watched him jog down the sidewalk and catch up with his friends, and for a moment she regretted blowing him off. And when Patrick and his friends had strolled out of view, she continued to stand at the register, eyes glazed, thinking of his piercing blue eyes, his cute stammer. Another shiver of pleasure rippled through her.

In reality, though, she wasn't ready to let another man in, not just yet.

At least, that's what she thought.

❧ ♦ ❧

Dora, the restaurant owner, one of those large, horsey-look-ing women who are immediately identifiable as not only suit-able but desirable because of their extraordinary down-home country common sense, pulled Winter aside and said, "Are y'all friggen' nuts sayin' no t' a hunk like that? How long has it been since a real man looked at you like you were hot an' spicy chicken tenders like that man just did?"

Winter didn't reply. Dora stopped cleaning the food coun-ter, spread her hands wide, and leaned toward Winter, eyeing her straight on, waiting, with one eyebrow arched into a question mark. Winter gave that noncommittal shrug of her shoulders, glaring back, raising both her eyebrows and trying to hold back a smile, and said, "What?"

"Uh, uh. That's what I thought," Dora shot back, shaking her head and rolling her eyes. "Where's your mind at?" Dora put her cleaning rag down, pointed her finger at Winter, moved toward the pie and cake display case, and continued her rant, "—that man, he's different. I can tell . . . "

Winter held herself still for the entire span of two seconds before they both burst into laughter. Dora reached for the choc-olate cake, chuckling, and sliced off two healthy pieces, putting them on plates and pushing one over to Winter. Taking a bite and shaking her fork at Winter, Dora added, "Seriously, now . . . there's somethin' not right with you. You need to be gettin' on with the business of life—or at the least gettin' it on with that man."

Dora forked another chunk of cake, opened her mouth

and slowly slid it in, swallowed hard, and said, "You should be scrubbin' dishes with him, instead of settin'♦ here eatin' cake with a crusty-ole bird like me—if you know what I'm sayin'."

"Yeah, well—" Winter thought for a second, then replied, "—men always change once you get to know 'em. An' there ain't nothin' a gal can— "

Dora took another forkful of cake and interrupted with a humph. "My, my, you sure have a bee up your butt about men," and then she added right away, squinting one eye at Winter and wagging her fork again, "—with a lick an' a promise✗ that guy could be the one." They both smiled at each other, trying not to laugh again.

"I think you've had enough cake," Winter said as she took a nice large bite from her own slice—dark brown, gooey—and opened her mouth wide to get it all in.

"Yeah . . . well . . . Lord knows, it's nonna my business," Dora responded, preparing herself for another healthy mouthful and quickly added, "I say this and shut up. This here's one helluva cake but it don't beat havin' a good man warmin' up my four-poster at night, that's for sure."

⌘ ✦ ⌘

Winter was outgoing by nature and cautious by what life had taught her. But she felt Dora was right. For the first time in the longest time, Patrick was someone she could fall for—and she knew it. It rattled her. A lot. And, in a way, Winter thought she might be ready for a little rattling. Well . . . maybe?

During the rest of the day when Winter thought about Patrick, she hoped, with all her heart, he would return like

♦*settin': The vernacular used in many rural areas of southern Indiana for "sitting."*
✗*lick an' a promise: A colloquialism used in many rural areas of southern Indiana that is an expression for a "hope and a prayer" or "with a little luck."*

he said he would. Each time she held his image in her mind, she smiled, and each time Dora caught Winter smiling, Dora would ask, "Why you grinnin' like that?" and Winter would reply, "No reason—just grinnin'." And they would humph, or laugh at each other.

Dora was a bright spot.

A true blessing.

A valuable friend, and the perfect sounding board. Someone she could rely on and someone she could turn to when dark shadows followed her, and she felt troubled.

෨ ♦ ෫

When Winter's father passed away, she had learned to be more than capable around the farm. She could do almost anything that needed to be done, and if she couldn't, she wasn't too proud to ask a neighbor for help.

And when she and Ben had been together, she'd become used to the rhythm of married life. After his death, she'd been forced to do everything for herself again.

She found she had forgotten how to do it.

Couldn't face it.

Didn't want to face it.

But the farm had molded her personality and had given her a strong character and made her resilient—even though, for a while, she lost her way.

Now, though, when she thought about her marriage to Ben, she knew that she and Ben had settled. Partly because she believed neither of them had had the guts to look any further—afraid there wasn't anyone better out in the world—and also because maybe they had become complacent and, in a way, they had taken one another for granted.

She had tried to convince herself, while she'd been married to Ben, that settling and becoming complacent was what adults did. And only after Ben did his deep dive into the abyss did she decide she'd been with the wrong man from the get-go. Yes, a man she liked and had respected and loved before he got all crazy on her. But now she understood Ben hadn't been her right partner in life. That man might still be out there somewhere.

At least, that's what she hoped.

Getting Frankie out of her life was a big step forward. And once again she was on her own. This time, however, things hadn't been all that difficult, stressful perhaps but nothing that would knock her to her knees. In many ways, the choices she was making now in her life had actually become a challenge she was enjoying—going back to school, being a waitress again, meeting new friends, and of course, helping Chelsea adapt to their new surroundings.

But dating, that was an entirely different animal. The very word "dating" filled her with fear. But Winter had to admit, she did miss the affection of a man. Intimacy. Feeling safe and walking through life unafraid with someone she trusted.

॰ ◆ ॰

Patrick had been true to his word. He returned to the diner and went back for lunch the very next day, and the day after that. Each time when he paid the check at the cash register, he would formally introduce himself and ask Winter to have dinner with him. Whatever it took.

Each time he'd ask her to dinner, she would hand back his receipt and respectfully decline. He would smile, and say, "I'll see you tomorrow." Dora was standing a little behind Winter and gave Patrick a toothy grin and a wink. He thought it best to be polite, as was his nature, and smiled back, but didn't wink.

On Patrick's third attempt, Winter did not refuse. Patrick's persistence and his straightforward and confident manner persuaded her to accept. Not to mention the fact that Dora would whip her redheaded fanny if she didn't. Mostly, though, the pleasing shiver she had each time she was near Patrick convinced her to say yes to his invitation.

"Lunch only," she said. "Here at the diner." Patrick smiled, and Winter could feel her face flush as fiery red as the color of her hair. If she allowed herself, she could become utterly attached to this guy. But she pushed aside that pleasurable warm rush. *Why waste a good glow if the guy turns out to be a jerk*, she thought. *Never, again.*

ॐ ♦ ॐ

Winter believed one day she would find her prince. She knew it was a silly notion to have that thought, especially in the era of the liberated women. She wasn't stupid. She read Beauvoir's book *The Second Sex*. But she still had hope.

She accepted that her man didn't need to ride a white stallion; he just needed to be a truthful, sincere, loving man—and mentally healthy. That wasn't too much to ask for, she thought. The big question running through her mind was: *Was Patrick the real deal?* As easy as it was to instantly like Patrick, she was going to make damn sure he wasn't a nutcase. Or like most men who have one thing on their mind, and only one thing, before realizing becoming good friends first is far better than any one-night stand could ever be.

Or maybe he was a soup-slurper.

Slurping she wouldn't put up with—at all.

On the other hand, she thought, if Patrick turned out to be what he *appeared* to be, maybe slurping wouldn't be so bad. *Chicken soup*, she said to herself, *We'll have chicken soup for lunch.*

☙ ✦ ❧

Their lunch together—slurping chicken soup together—was cordial and enjoyable. They found a natural fluidity with their conversations. One of the many things Winter found refreshing with Patrick was that he didn't ask any questions about her past. Which was a pleasant surprise, and thoroughly added to his charm. And one of the many things about Winter Patrick found refreshing was that she asked a lot of questions.

It had been Winter who stepped up and invited Patrick to a dinner date. Regardless of how easy it was for her to be with Patrick, she still believed she had to keep her vulnerability in check. She was smart enough to be careful. Plus, there was always a terrible feeling skulking inside her that things might fall to pieces. Or she might lose her direction again. Or another lightning strike might be lurking just around the corner.

It didn't take much time at all for Winter to realize that, with Patrick, if she told him she only wanted to be friends, he would unequivocally respect her plea and abide by it. She decided she'd take a chance with Patrick, but not without promising herself to keep a watchful eye out for any suspicious or tilted psychological issues. So, just to be safe, the first thing she asked Patrick on their first lunch date was: *"Do you have any emotional disorders or tattoos?"*

She was pleased to find that he had neither.

Not only did they continue to have lunches and dinners with each other, they also had picnics with Chelsea.

Chelsea, like Winter, held guarded emotions. But Chelsea also had been taken by the careful, respectful manner in which Patrick treated her and how funny and fun he was to be around.

✦

Patrick's time away from his work went by in a flash. After he left Indiana to go back to Kentucky, every weekend, all summer long without fail, he would return to Bloomington to visit his family and spend time with Winter and Chelsea.

The connection between Winter and Patrick had grown rapidly. More importantly, Bill and Maureen and Dan had opened up their hearts and their home to Winter and Chelsea as well.

Being with Patrick changed Winter's life in the best way possible. It wasn't only about softening her sheltered feelings. It was how connected Patrick had become with Chelsea. It was incredible to see Chelsea relate to a man so cheerfully and not be afraid. Winter was beginning to feel as if Patrick could become her safety net. A man who could protect her and her daughter and keep them safe, who treated her as an equal, respected her and truly listened to what she had to say. This, she thought, was what a relationship should feel like. A stunning breathless *rightness* she never expected.

ॐ ◆ ॐ

When she thought of Ben now, she only had kind thoughts
of him. For the longest time, she thought she had failed Ben because she had given up trying to help him. She had blamed herself for that and let "*what if*" and "*if only*" invade her thoughts
on a regular basis: *What if I had been more understanding? If only I
had seen the signs . . .*

But she forgave him and realized that for whatever reason
he couldn't choose otherwise. It wasn't entirely his fault, and
it certainly wasn't her fault, but she would never forget. She
would always think kindly of Ben from now on, but her world
would forever be colored by his suicide.

She also forgave Frankie for being the ass that he was, because she knew he could never be anything else but an ass—it
was his nature. Actually, she felt like thanking Frankie. As far
as she was concerned, if it hadn't been for him, she wouldn't
have moved to Bloomington and would never have met Patrick.

At least with Patrick, she had the possibility of a robust and
positive future with a man who was conscientious, monoga-
mous, emotionally stable, and on top of all that, had a good
job. What could be better than that, when it came to a man?

ॐ ◆ ॐ

Whatever choice Winter made from this point on would
decisively determine her pursuit of happiness. She had been
so consumed with day-to-day life, she'd almost forgotten the
things she enjoyed before she became a wife, a mother, and a
widow. Things that fed her soul. Simple things, like planting

flowers in a garden, quiet talks with her daughter, and being truly loved and cared for by a wonderful man. She and Patrick were happy together, and he was devotion times two.

But there were occasional flickers of doubt—mementos left to her by Ben and Frankie. She knew Patrick was nothing like Ben and Frankie. No comparison on any scale whatsoever. Yet, there were times when she'd see a shadow walk across Patrick's face, or a comment he'd say during a discussion that would trigger a worry within her that she'd try to quiet and push aside.

It was inevitable she would struggle with the mirthless spirits of her past.

❧ ◆ ❧

Winter wanted so much to trust Patrick—with all her heart. When they were together, everything about the lightning strikes she'd endured would rise to the surface. And just when she thought she could tell him, she'd stop herself.

She knew every relationship was a gamble and was hard work. There were no guaranteed outcomes when loving someone so completely, zero certainties, good, bad, or indifferent. There was no pledge powerful enough that could promise a life with a partner would be forever. There was only the hope and determination to try the very best to make the magic of a partnership flourish.

One might say Patrick was Winter's fourth lightning strike. Not in a bad way. More like the lightning strike in Mary Shelley's Frankenstein that gave the monster new life. It did the same for Winter, giving her a chance for a new life, a new beginning.

She loved how Patrick made things fun and exciting and mysterious—made her laugh. When Patrick held her in his arms and kissed her with a soft touch on the lips, somewhere in Winter's brain a part of her responded instinctively to his touch. A stirring inside. A feeling she thought she'd lost.

Hope.

$\hat{\gamma} \bullet \hat{\gamma}$

Once in a while when Patrick held Winter in his arms, he could tell her mind would drift off somewhere far away, and when they'd kiss, he could feel her hold back her kiss, and her body would tense.

During those moments, he wouldn't be inquisitive and pry, just gently hold her, until she relaxed and let the tension escape. It was easy to sense she wasn't ready to tell him everything about her past. *She's vulnerable*, he'd told himself in an effort to hold his feelings back, *and one should never tread on ground that's soft and fragile.*

He could wait.

He adored her.

He most certainly could wait.

Patrick believed that one time in a man's life he will realize what he wants more than anything else in the world. This much he did know: he would be pretending to be happy with anyone else other than Winter—always living a lie—and Patrick never lied to himself about anything, especially about love. *If a man was lucky*, he said to himself, *a man would move toward the right woman without even trying.*

He had no idea what on earth he had done to deserve a woman like Winter, but he wasn't going to cross-examine his good luck. He would take it for what it was: *plain good luck.* As simple as that. Just plain good luck.

❧ ◆ ❧

There are significant moments that occur in our lives which are permanently recorded in our minds—moments we will never forget, like landing on the moon, for instance—that mark our lives so much so that whatever happens from that point on will forever be changed.

For Patrick, meeting Winter was one of those moments. In the short time Patrick and Winter had been together, Patrick could tell his life had indeed changed, and he knew his life would continue to change—change for the better, as long as he had Winter. He sensed it, in the same way people's hips, elbows, and knees can feel the onset of a thunderstorm hours before it arrives.

Unlike Winter, Patrick was not afraid of lightning. Without even trying, she had solidly branded herself on his heart, and just the thought of not being with her seemed unimaginable. Patrick had been hoping for a woman like Winter his entire life.

He knew it the first time he looked into her green eyes and felt her soft lips embrace his, inviting him, challenging him to get to know her. He was falling for her hard and fast. And he liked how it made him feel. It made him feel complete. Loved. Added a higher purpose to his life. And he, too, like Winter, felt the delicious sweet taste of hope.

There was no doubt about it.
Patrick was falling for Winter with all his heart,
and he had no intention of stopping the fall.

*Once we open our hearts to the magic of things,
things happen . . .*

Excerpts from the author's journal, On The Road.

—Late Evening, Sunday, April 05, 1987

Still in Utah.
Up in the mountains at Sundance camping.
I often find myself under the stars gazing in absolute wonderment.
So many stars and yet,
there is so much empty space between them all.
What the heck is out there?
My thoughts always jump into another and when they do,
I can't help but think of my Martha.

· · ·

— Friday, May 15, 1987

What a great week this week has been.
I did two mime performances in elementary schools.
Oh my, how I love to hear children laugh when I mime.
I had the honor of doing three large abstract paintings
for one of the schools.
We set up the canvases in the gym, and I painted a landscape
abstract (while the students watched), of the mountains
that protect and look over their school.
Then I had each child put their thumb in different colors of paint,
and planted their thumbprints right on the paintings for the flowers.
The kids had a blast, and the principle hung the paintings in the
front entryway of the school.
What a wonderful memory for everyone.
Made me feel really good.
Proud.

CHAPTER V

One Starry Night

Wednesday, February 14
Early Morning: 3 AM – Couldn't sleep.
Made a grilled cheese, tomato, and bacon sandwich,
with chips and a Pepsi.
Valentine's Day.
I will write another letter to my
Martha before I let the day drift away
and dream of her tonight as I sleep . . .

One weekend evening together at Winter's rented home, Patrick, Winter, and Chelsea were having the grandest time trying to make sushi for dinner, which in turn made eating their odd-shaped sushi rolls all the more fun to devour. After dinner, they decided they wanted to do some stargazing and drove out to the large field at the highest point in Brown County State Park.

The open-air pasture greeted them with a broad, moonless

sky. Grasshoppers, mixed with crickets and cicadas, played their night sonatas, and owls took turns, adding their calls to the evening symphony.

The air was cool but gentle. With a big comfy blanket on the ground and pillows for their heads, they neatly lined themselves up in a row. They gazed up, all set for the stars to come out, and shine—a perfect evening for stargazing.

At the edge of the field, where the forest line made its stand, the bright dome of sky was fading as the sun silently walked down behind the trees, with leaves turning and fluttering from twilight's dusky breath. Winter's hair soaked up the sunset, adding an electric aura along the edges as the cool evening breeze played with the unruly strands of it, which gently fell on her shoulders.

❧ ◆ ❧

The three of them stretched out on the blanket watched the stars silently blink to life, their light coruscating out of the black and shimmering as if millions of light switches were being flicked on one by one. Soon, all the sunlight would give way to the night, and the entire cosmic expanse would be carpeted with twinkling lights from horizon to horizon.

Patrick couldn't help but smile and sigh. A good sigh. A sigh of contentment and relief. Relief that he found someone extraordinary. Someone he could share his private thoughts with. He closed his eyes and imagined how everyone was winding down from their daytime activities, cars tucked away in garages or parked up next to the curb, TVs turned on, illuminating living rooms and bedrooms. Everyone waiting for sleep to take them to another day. He could almost hear the hush of the night telling those who cared to listen, time to let go the worries and stress of the day and sleep in peace. And there he was, next to Winter.

He opened his eyes. Turned his head to look at Winter. He inched over and gently pressed his shoulder to her shoulder. He thought about all the things he sensed in her: kindness, charity, passion. He was drawn to her, pulled by some mysterious, seductive magnet. Being next to her warm body on a brisk stargazing night was just perfect, and Patrick knew, without a doubt, he wanted to be with her for the rest of his life. He could tell she was drawn to him, too, by the same force but he was also aware she was fighting with intimacy, pushing it back, keeping it just under the surface.

He had not tried to shower her with his own ardent desires; he had sensed that if he had done so, the spark she had for him might lessen. At times she reminded him of a wounded or abused animal, hesitant to trust anyone, shy, but gravely wanting to open up and feel the hug of affection and rely on someone unconditionally.

Patrick gently rubbed a single finger along her palm. A tiny movement, one could easily miss. But it was like an invisible electric shock connecting them together. Winter slid her hand into his and gently squeezed, her delicate fingers laced with his. He had never experienced such a soothing, comforting sensation with any other woman he had ever dated, until now.

"Thank you for forcing me to be your boyfriend," Patrick whispered, looking up at the sky.

"My pleasure," Winter whispered back, squeezing his hand

tighter. "Glad I could knock some sense into you."

ᵰ ◆ ᵱ

Patrick had always believed he could predict—to some degree—how his life was going to unfold, but he never imaged he would meet someone like Winter. *Our lives are merely a collection of memories, like the click of a camera,* Patrick thought as he turned his head to look at Winter, and then rolled his head in the opposite direction to look at Chelsea. *Photos taken of each moment that passes before our eyes.* All Patrick wanted was to enjoy every picture he and Winter could paint together. *Because, in the end,* he thought, *all we have left are the photos we make of our lives.*

On rare occasions, after Chelsea had gone to bed early, they would cuddle and fall asleep together on Winter's couch. He could always tell when she was about to fall asleep because she would start to twitch. First, her fingers in her right hand would make a quick tiny jump.

Then, a second later her left hand would jerk harder. Then her foot, elbow, fingers, and then her leg would twitch—always random. Some were barely noticeable, while others so vigorous they'd jolt her awake, and she'd say in a slow, drowsy voice, "Did I just twitch?" Patrick would wait, wait in the silence, wait for the moment, and watch until she closed her eyes and drifted back to sleep.

The twitching was irresistibly adorable, and when she found her sleeping rhythm, her twitching stopped, and he'd listen to the slow, soft, unconscious tempo of each breath she took, until he drifted off, too.

One night, before Winter fell asleep in Patrick's arms, he

asked her, hesitantly, "What happened to you, Winter?" His face pinched with concern.

Her eyes met his and looked straight into him, and he wanted to drown in the green looking back. He was only beginning to understand how to read her expressions and thought he saw surprise staring back at him, maybe a glint of romance, but he also saw fear—of that he was sure.

Fear of him? Maybe?

Fear of his love? Most likely?

But it seemed to be so much more than all that.

Patrick realized he had triggered something, and her eyes pooled. She blinked a couple of times, a tear escaped at the edge of her eye, followed by more. She blinked again as if clearing away too many thoughts and then wiped away the tears with the back of her hand. She could not stop the memories from rolling over her, and her eyes became misty again, with remembered sadness and helplessness. Her words caught in her throat and came out as a whispered chant, "Thank you for comin' into my life," she said.

"I'll stay till you fall asleep," Patrick replied in a soft tone. She closed her eyes. Patrick kissed her brow, each eyelid, and the freckles on her cheeks, drinking in her tears and held her in his arms until the twitching started again.

ॐ ◆ ॐ

The last bit of rusty rose-colored sunglow pushed through the tree line. It thinned to a faint transparent pinkish hue and washed away, surrendering to the black as the trees disappeared into dark relief against the diminishing curtain of pastel.

Fireflies pranced in and out of the trees, blinking off and on as if the stars had come down from heaven.

Patrick loved the sounds of the night and the frailty of the dusk afterglow, especially when the blazing scarlet calmed itself down to a rusty color. And when the cooling light highlighted Winter's red hair, it made her skin glow and her startling green eyes shine even brighter. Now he could add Winter to the list of the many things he found singularly notable about dusk before the black swallowed the light.

Such a tranquil scene made Patrick wish fleeting moments, like that moment, under a star-studded night sky with two people he cared for, would continue indefinitely. *If only a person were cunning enough to stop time,* he thought.

꩜ ◆ ꩜

Winter had always hoped and prayed one day the tragedies that followed her would move on and settle into comfortable obscurity. The years had changed her. Not all that much physically—although a close observer would notice the tiny lines that sorrow had etched around her eyes.

Each time she and Patrick were together (especially at that moment when laying on the ground and watching the night sky with his hand touching hers), she sincerely believed as if she could let the details of her past dissolve into nothing more than a nameless unknown fable. Little had been left that could make her feel attractive anymore—or alluring, or desirable, she thought. That hadn't always been the case, although if it couldn't be said that she had expectations years ago, it could be said that she possessed dreams to be loved again, truly loved.

Patrick made her feel pretty again. He made all those mouth-watering seductive romantic desires she thought she had lost, bubble to the surface. When that happened, her mind would drift away with little or no effort into bliss, as she dreamed and fantasized that . . . well . . . just fantasized. She wanted to tell Patrick everything in that breathless, confiding, private whisper, after lovemaking. She knew it would be a simple thing to let go and open herself to him. Each time she rested her head on his shoulder, and Patrick held her gently in his arms, her heart buzzed and throbbed in her chest like honey bees preening their queen.

At the same time, Patrick frightened her.

Not a lot. Only a little.

Perhaps it was because he was such a good man; perhaps because Chelsea adored him; perhaps because she adored him too. Or maybe because Patrick possessed all the qualities she found so appealing and exciting in a man—qualities she always wanted in a man.

She saw him as someone who knew precisely what was inside his heart, and she could tell he would refuse to pretend otherwise. Always candid and open with his feelings, simple as that. A trait of his that she most admired.

Well, that, and the way he kissed.

The way Patrick kissed her was a trait rare to most men. Just thinking of his kisses made her neck tingle and her body quiver. A man had never kissed her the way Patrick kissed her. Most men believe kissing is using their tongue as a dental probe, without any more feeling for their sexual desires than a dentist exploring for cavities.

Not Patrick.

He would reach for her face first, touching her skin lightly. He'd stroke her cheek and let his fingers brush across her lips, eyes open, committed. Then he'd cup her chin, skim his thumb down its shallow dent, and brush his mouth over hers, creating a dance of expectation. And when Patrick's soft lips moved slowly, gently pressing onto hers, it was as if he were melting into her flesh. Then, his tongue would find hers but touch only for a second. And when he pulled back, he would gently tug and pull her lower lip, at the same time giving a tiny, sharp but tender bite to release her, which sent shock waves all through her.

That's all it took.

It awakened her.

It was that immediate, staggering lift of her heart. Patrick's touch spoke to her with a seductive, powerful desire; she couldn't help herself. "Yes" was the word she tried to say each time he kissed her, but it only came out as a muffled, pleasurable moan, torn deep from her throat. And she yielded—when someone kisses you with everything they feel from the very depth of their soul, it stays with you. It's a kiss to remember for a lifetime.

Winter's skin was sensitive, ultra-sensitive. It had been such a long time since a man touched her, and everywhere Patrick reached, it tingled—raising the hair on the back of her neck. She wanted his touch to wipe everything away—Ben, Frankie, losing the farm—everything.

She'd almost forgotten what it was like to feel the flash of heat with a man or to be caressed and have strong, steady hands persuading her. She'd almost forgotten the thrill and the sheer excitement that can grow to a boiling point to where it drives you crazy. But it was more than the flash of heat that comes with a relationship new and exciting.

Everything about Patrick felt right.

So much so, it was almost painful.

❧ ◆ ❧

For some beautiful reason, that night the sky had an ample supply of falling stars streaking and skipping across the black. Each one they saw left streaks of white, made them gasp and shout and point.

It was all wonderfully exciting, and the three of them together encouraged each other to let the excitement spill out unfettered. Such a starry show. They saw more shooting stars than they could count zipping through the Milky Way. Patrick, a true romantic, told the ladies to make a wish on each and every star that fell that night. They all made a lot of wishes that night, laughed, and drank in the love that was tying them together.

❧ ◆ ❧

The next day, the three of them decided it would be fun to take a short road trip, traveling the back roads as Patrick loved to do, down to Marengo Cave in southern Indiana. Patrick had been there as a child and thought it would be an excellent adventure for Chelsea to experience. He loved the feeling of a road trip and exploring because one never knew what exciting events might cross one's path. It was a perfect day for a drive: sunny and warm, but not too warm. They stopped at old churches along the way to take photos and posed in front of gentle rolling hay fields spotted with round fresh-cut bales.

In the small town of Salem, Indiana, as they were driving around its town square with its turnoff roads connecting like spokes on a wheel, they noticed that one of the side-street buildings had a boldly painted abstract mural on its wall. In some ways out of character for a small town, but most definitely another perfect photo opportunity. As they pulled into an open parking space, another car, a red, sleek 1960 Ford Falcon compact, parked in the open spot right next to them.

Patrick didn't think much of it at the time, except the driver, an older gentleman, did have trouble centering his Falcon between the white lines but more or less, angled his way into position.

Patrick, Winter, and Chelsea approached the mural-clad wall and began their photo session. But Patrick noticed that the older gentleman who'd parked next to his car had magically appeared on the opposite side of the street corner. For how long, Patrick didn't know. He was standing there, smiling, watching.

The old dude was bent over from age and had a lean, lanky body, with long thin arms, spindly as a praying mantis, and a face full of robust features, etched from years of experience. He was maybe in his early eighties—still hale and hardy—eyes filled with kindness. His long arms hung awkwardly at his sides, and his knuckles on his hands were gnarled as old branches on an apple tree.

He was wearing a fishing hat that had seen better days, a

plaid shirt, and a pair of good old-fashioned, down-home bib overalls that came down just above his ankle-high boots showing his white cotton socks.

Clouds were rolling in, being pushed by a strong wind. On the ground the gusts were moderate, but the temperature was falling. *Could be a storm brewing*, Patrick said to himself looking at the darker sky in the west, *or just the threat of one*. He turned his head and watched the old guy do a small, lanky, elbow gesture wave. Patrick hesitantly returned the same casual wave, and the old dude did an old-dude-bunny-hop off the curb and said, "Have y'all ever seen a meteorite?" while he navigated across the street toward Patrick.

"Sorry?" Patrick yelled back, cupping his ear, as the old man's words were taken by the wind.

"M-e-t-e-o-r!" the old guy voiced louder. "Have you'ens❖ ever seen a meteorite?" He extended his hand to Patrick.

"Yes, I have," Patrick said in a softer voice, carefully shaking the man's twisted, arthritic hand and thinking it was an odd question to ask. "I'm Patrick. This is Winter—and Chelsea."

"My name's Fred," he said and tipped his fishing hat to Winter. "Fred Reed." He hesitated, mesmerized by Winter's emerald eyes. "Ma'am. Tis a pleasure." And then Fred looked down at Chelsea, bent forward enough to look her in the eye, too, tipped his hat again and said, "Little miss. Tis a pleasure, for sure . . . Would you'ens like to see a meteorite? I got a bunch in the trunk of my car." He winked at Chelsea and smiled again. Chelsea smiled back and shook her head and looked at Patrick for approval.

"Sure, why not," Patrick said. Then Patrick thought: *What*

the heck is this crazy old dude doing? Is he going to try and sell us some rock he dug out of his backyard? They followed Fred back to his car out of sheer curiosity. And then Patrick added, "Where you from, Fred?"

"Lived here in Salem my whole life," Fred replied, as they sauntered down the sidewalk, and then he said, "My wife, Agatha—well—we never did have no children. Should've did that when we wuz first married. Anyway, we wuz settin' out on our porch last night—been married fifty-two years we have— an' anyway, we wuz settin' out on the porch watchin' the sun go down an' lookin' all them real pretty pinks an' orange collars◆ spillin' out all over everywhere."

Fred stopped walking and turned to look at his followers and added, "We had all the lights off in the house so we could do some star countin'. . . we love doin' that together, takin' a look-see at all them twinkles on a clear night." He pulled a handkerchief from his back pocket, blew his nose (belted out a good one), folded it and put it back in his back pocket and continued, "Anyway, we wuz so 'xcited an' saw so many fallin' stars we thought our jaws wuz gonna git stuck wide open, like a couple of coyots a howlin' at the moon—"

"We saw that too!" Chelsea interrupted excitedly.

" . . . I love them coyots when they be a singin' at the night," Fred continued. "It curdles the blood, don't ya think?" Then he winked at Chelsea. "But them meteors—now, that wuz some-thin' special it wuz—zoomin' 'round from one end of the sky t' the other . . . Anyway . . ."

ॐ ◆ ॐ

◆*collars: The vernacular used in many rural areas of southern Indiana for "colors."*

Patrick loved everything about Chelsea, especially at that very moment seeing the excitement rush across her eyes with Fred's story about the meteorite. There was something magical about watching Chelsea so enthralled by the mystery of the unknown unraveling right before her eyes, Patrick thought.

Chelsea was so full of energy, so inquisitive, and so beautiful, exactly like her mom with alabaster skin and flaming red hair. It didn't surprise Patrick at all how easily Chelsea had become interlaced into his life. Chelsea would ask questions that no one else would dare to: *Do lawyers put people in jail? Does it bother you when you put them in jail? Are you going to marry my mom?* Patrick didn't try and avoid any of Chelsea's questions because he knew she wouldn't stop asking until she got the answer she was digging for. He knew precisely where she picked up that distinguishing quality. Chelsea was, without a doubt, in many ways, Winter's twin.

Throughout Patrick's adult life, the idea of being a father, the joy of seeing your own child you created with the one you loved, was a tad terrifying. Exciting, yes, but terrifying. A responsibility so huge the mere idea overwhelmed Patrick.

Until he met Chelsea.

Not having a father had been something Patrick did know about and understood completely. This common ground connected Patrick and Chelsea and helped him realize the father he could become.

He loved watching Chelsea percolate with unspoiled anticipation. Seeing the sparkle of wonder dance in her eyes was equally infectious, as was her unbridled enthusiasm and eagerness to learn about the world around her. *Another pleasant memory for later on in life,* Patrick thought.

ॐ ◆ ॐ

"*We didn't hear* any coyots," Chelsea said, her excitement spilling over, animated and uninhibited. "But we did see fallin' stars shootin' across the sky every which way."

"Oh, my!" Fred responded, making eye contact with Chelsea with kind eyes. He lifted one scraggy eyebrow. "You saw them fallin' stars too?" He bent over slightly, leaning closer to Chelsea and continued his story adding slowly and carefully, "A-n-y-w-a-y, suddenly there wuz this really, really, *really* bright flash. It wuz so bright Agatha an' me, we had to cover our eyes, an' then—whoosh. It flew right over the top of our house." As Fred spoke, he waved his hand to imitate the whooshing sound of the meteorites. "I knowed 'xactly what it wuz."

Chelsea's eyebrows arched up. "Then *BOOM!*" Fred bellowed, spreading his arms out as far as he could stretch them, looking like a long-legged, long-armed alien, and said, "Somethin' crashed right into our vegetable garden—'bout knocked Agatha an' me right outta our rockin' chairs. Agatha thought it'd be a good ideal◆ to git us inside. She was 'fraid somethin' fierce. I weren't. I ain't 'fraid of nothin'." Chelsea's eyes were wide open, and Fred added, "Anyway, it was a sight. A real sight fir sure. There in the vegetable garden wuz where I found them four meteorites." He opened the trunk of his car and there, resting on an old raggedy bath towel, were four fist-sized lumps of celestial rock. "An' you know what?" Fred continued, "Them darn meteors were so dad-blamed hot they cooked all our veggies in our garden." Then he paused a beat, as if trying to catch

◆*ideal: The vernacular used in many rural areas of southern Indiana for "idea."*

a thought, and winked at Patrick and Winter, grinned at Chelsea, and added, "Yup, hot steamed vegetables were lettin' out steam everywhere. Good tastin', too." Fred picked up one the meteorites from the trunk of his car and handed it to Chelsea.

"It's so heavy," Chelsea said, her eyes saucer-like, entirely mesmerized by Fred and his meteorites. As Chelsea cradled the stone in her hands, Fred held out a small magnet a couple of inches away from the side of the meteorite. He let it go. The magnet was pulled instantly to the iron stone as if the rock itself reached out and snatched the magnet out of Fred's fingers. Chelsea smiled as if the sun had bloomed across her face. No question in Chelsea's mind the ironstone was magical, and Fred was a magician.

"I was thinkin' 'bout maybe you'd like t' be havin' this," Fred said smiling, as he handed one of the meteorites to Chelsea. Chelsea looked at her mother for permission.

Patrick said to Chelsea, "It's a rare moment when we can wish upon a falling star one dark and dreamy night, and the next day, hold that star in our hands and make a wish all over again." Then he looked at Fred, smiled, shook his hand and said, "Thanks, Fred. Really kind of you."

It was easy to like Fred. It didn't matter if the story he was telling was true or not. The man was harmless and loved to tell a tale, especially when the tellin' was about him and his wife Agatha, and he certainly had an affinity for using the word "anyway."

A-n-y-w-a-y, Patrick believed a person's life was not branded on their soul from the time they were born. Destiny, he thought, was like a cloud in the sky that has no choice in which way the wind will take it. But if you're willing to sail along, who knows what marvelous adventures would be in front for you.

੭ ◆ ੭

No one can predict his or her future. We can only dream of what it might become. Sometimes, unique and unexplained moments of inertia touch our lives. These one-of-a-kind occurrences can be unassuming little episodes that make us tilt our heads to one side and question why, and what could it possibly mean. Or they can be traumatic and horrifying experiences that make us snap our heads a lot harder, and cry out: Oh my dear God, why?

I often question what might happen if my alarm clock didn't go off as it does every morning. Maybe I'd be late for work, and as I'm walking up the sidewalk to enter my workplace, I'd watch a jetliner slam into the building, destroying it—girders and glass, rubble to ground. Or perhaps, I'd arrive at work right on time, and I'm typing a memo on the computer to all the employees not to forget the surprise birthday party for the boss at 3 PM. Then in a blink, the building is ripped apart by that jetliner, leaving nothing behind but nightmares and ash.

Perhaps things happen for a reason?

Or perhaps, life is purely a strange vagary of fate?

Maybe there is no such thing as coincidence?

Then again, maybe, just maybe, life is one big crazy remarkable accident?

We could be compelled to look at randomness and not see it as the absence of order, but rather as the presence of the unpredictable, that defines how our lives will unfold. Given enough time, anything and everything will happen at some point—this, I believe is an absolute.

The fact is, randomness, chaos, order, coincidence, it means nothing to the everyday Joe or Sally like you and me. All that randomness and chaos—all that abstract stuff, well, it's better left for scientists and mathematicians to figure out.

We cannot choose how our life will begin. We can, however, choose what we do with our lives once we realize that choice and consequence go hand and hand.

When real love kisses your heart
it is a kiss you will remember a lifetime
even when fate has determined
you will never kiss your true love again
or hold her in your arms
or listen to the rhythm of her heartbeat.
It is still a kiss you will remember forever
till death do you part . . .

Excerpts from the author's journal, On The Road.

— *Monday, April 04, 1988*

Moved to Hollywood. Smoggy. Tons of snarled traffic.
I've been living in Malibu, right on the beach, which helps ease
the stress of dealing with a city the likes of LA that feels so heartless.
Auditioned, and was accepted for acting lessons at the
Lee Strasberg Theatre Institute. My favorite acting coach was Sally
Kirkland. We've become friends. What stories I could write about
Sally. Sally invited Sam Shepard to a class and I did a scene from
one of his plays, Cowboy Mouth. He said I understood the character
and liked how I took the peaches from the can and spread them all over
my body. He told me he wrote it that way to cancel out inhibition.
What an interesting person. Not sure the peach juice canceled out any of
my inhibitions, though . . . felt sticky and uncomfortable by the end of
the scene. Maybe that was the point, letting go of inhibitions is uncomfortable.

— Saturday, April 09, 1988

Sally invited me over to her house for a writers workshop with a few of her Hollywood friends, including Sam Shepard. We each had to bring a manuscript we were working on and read a section from it for a critique. I read an outline for a novel I might write someday. Afterwords, Sam talked to me and said, "One day, you won't know why or how come, but one day, slick, an uncontrollable force will grab you by the balls and you'll write that novel. But for now, fuck it. Have another drink."

.   .   .

— Friday, February 24, 1989

Went to an open casting call today.
I got the part.
Believe it or not, as a mime.
But this mime spoke and said three words, "Go to hell!" right in the face of Robert Urich.
I guess I said it like I meant it.
He didn't like it all that much and complained to the director. Said I wasn't supposed to be upset when I told him to go to hell? Really? I didn't care, saying those three words was enough to get my SAG card.
How crazy is that!
I'm leaving, though.
Hate it here.
Maybe Hawaii?
I'll miss working with Sally!

CHAPTER VI

Turning Into a Pumpkin

Thursday, March 08
Early Morning: First birdsongs,
Almost finished writing about Winter.
Makes me wonder where my Martha is,
and what she is doing at this very moment.
I hope she found her heaven.
If God allows it, one day I will see her again . . .

*I*t *had been* on Patrick's last weekend visit, during the middle of September before his big case, that he invited Winter to accompany him to his law firm's annual Halloween masked ball. Not your everyday dress-up Halloween costume party, mind you, but a real, formal ball, with men in tuxes and ladies in gowns, and all who attend wearing masks.

"It's the firm's annual Halloween dance at the end of October," Patrick said. Before she even had a chance to respond, Patrick pulled Winter toward him and started slow dancing, and added, "I have to warn you. I'm afraid I'm not a very good dancer. I rock back and forth standing in one place really well, though." Patrick reached around Winter's waist with both arms and gently eased her into him, bodies as one. He sighed in satisfaction, tracing the delicate planes of Winter's soft cheeks with a loving eye. Speaking in her ear with guarded breath, he said, "You can lock your arms around my neck, and we can sway together mask to mask."

"What about Chelsea. She can't stay alone?" she whispered back.

"I've already asked a buddy of mine and his wife. They're going to the dance, too, and they'll have a reliable babysitter for their two kids. They said they'd love to have Chelsea." And then Patrick added, "You and Chelsea can come down for the weekend. We'll do some fun things during the day—it'll be nice."

"I don't have a dress for that kinda fancy, shindig." Winter blanched, her voice edgy, wrinkling her forehead with concern. "I don't know—and you know I can't spend the money on somethin' like that." She knew it wasn't about the dress or the money. *I'm not a swan*, she thought. *Everyone will know I don't fit in with his crowd. They'll see right through me. It'll be a disaster. I'll make a fool of myself and embarrass him.*

"You don't need to decide now. There's no hurry. I thought if you wanted to go with me . . . ," Patrick said, rubbing Winter's shoulders, conscious she had tightened. Then he added with hopeful eyes, "I mean, since the ball is Sunday evening we'd have Saturday to do whatever . . . I know this great deli where we can have lunch. You'll love it. And I can show you where I grew up as a kid . . . We'll buy a dress—if you'll let me—maybe some shoes to match? Make a day of it—it'll be fun."

But Winter couldn't say yes and told him she didn't feel comfortable about going to a formal dance.

As disappointing as it was for Patrick, he understood her fears and didn't bring the subject up again. He cupped her chin in the palm of his hand, urging her lips toward his and thinking, *A face as pretty as Winter's should never be wrinkled in worry.*

After Patrick left that weekend, she hated herself for saying no. It had not been a good way to say goodbye to each other, especially when it would be a while before Patrick would be able to take time off from work to visit because of the trial.

◈ ✦ ◈

Patrick had hoped to have Winter standing with him at the ball and to introduce her to everyone who worked at the firm.

He was sure his coworkers were tired of him talking about Winter all the time. Many teased him that she wasn't real, an apparition, a specter seducing him in his dreams. Or perhaps, undigested gruel causing hallucinations. Having his friends meet Winter would dispel any and all notions that she was a figment of his imagination.

On his drive back down to Louisville, he thought about everything that had happened that weekend. It had been a perfect weekend. An eye-opening weekend. And each time he thought about Winter, he'd smile. It didn't bother Patrick in the least that Winter didn't feel comfortable attending the dance. Disappointed a little, yes, but to Patrick, the Halloween party was no big deal. He was more surprised by the fact Winter continued to keep him at a distance because that weekend she had trusted him enough to tell him everything, from her parents' deaths to Ben's suicide—even about Frankie. In many ways, it was a breakthrough weekend, filled with a lot of healthy venting and bonding.

Patrick had said to her then:

> When you lose someone close to you, it feels like you've lost the whole world. And if you have to cry, then cry your heart out. Once you're done crying, though, you still have to live.
>
> At some point, a person realizes the world is still out there, waiting, and it's okay to love and be loved.

❧ ♦ ❧

From the moment Patrick had that first lunch date with Winter—slurping chicken soup together—Patrick sensed a connection, and it had strengthened every time they were together. He loved the way she fit perfectly in his arms and the way she'd twitch before she fell asleep. He loved her spirit and her fire, her tenderness, her vulnerability. And he loved her all the more for opening her heart enough for him to take a sympathetic peek inside. Although he was empathetic and eager to help Winter get past her troubles, in truth, none of the past mattered if she wasn't brave enough to knock out the demons that were trying to whittle her down a few sizes.

Patrick knew he could only help so much.

As far as he was concerned, things happen, and a person either moves on with their life, or they don't. Everyone has their own unique way when dealing with grief, and some just take longer to work through their pain than others. What mattered to Patrick was for Winter to let go of her past and move forward, so they could move forward together.

One day, he thought, she would peel off her past and throw it away. The line in the sand she had made for herself, the fear, the hopelessness, all of it would disappear once she found the moxie to step over it. He hoped she'd change her mind and join him at the ball. But he wasn't going to put down any bets on it.

❧ ✦ ❧

The rest of September and the entire month of October had been hectic for Patrick. Filled with hard work, stress, and frustration. Stress from the trial and frustration from not being able to visit Winter and Chelsea. Patrick could tell by Winter's tone when he talked to her on the phone that she was disappointed he couldn't make any trips to see her.

He didn't like it any better than she did, but there wasn't anything he could do about it. Litigation required eighteen-hour work days and lost weekends. In the end, however, the pressure and the sleepless nights all paid off. The trial ended sooner than anyone expected—all due to Patrick's attention to detail, his careful planning, and strong courtroom presence. The judge ruled in his favor (a healthy settlement for the client, and for the firm) and the next thing he knew, he received his promotion.

Winning the case, becoming a junior partner in the firm—the fra-la-la was intoxicating, if he allowed it. Patrick's practical nature made it easy for him to brush all the hoopla celebrating aside. He had a lot more important matters in his life that deserved his attention. Including a pile of paperwork and stacks of files sitting on his desk.

Yet, at the same time, Patrick had always wondered what it would feel like to stand on the podium at the Olympics. Raise both arms in the air, wave to the crowd, listen to the national anthem and have a gold medal hanging around his neck. He couldn't help but admit, being a winner felt good. Really good. Remarkably good. But as good as Patrick felt, he still didn't feel like celebrating. His happiness, the experience, all of it felt hollow without Winter to enjoy it with him. It was amazing to him how someone could fill the empty parts. Even more amazing to him, for the first time in his life, there was nothing left to fill.

He felt whole.

Yes, he was working hard to build a life for himself. A very good life. But that wasn't enough. He realized his job could never fill the bitter emptiness he lived with as an orphan. It wasn't difficult for Patrick to figure out what would make his life truly meaningful.

But now, he was working on a much bigger dream than just being a successful attorney. A dream that included Winter and Chelsea; a belief that their lives would be better because they would be together. He knew exactly what he needed to do next.

❧ ◆ ❧

When Winter's mind acted rationally and wasn't weighted down by apprehensiveness, she understood the reason Patrick couldn't make his usual visits to see her. She knew the month of October was a pivotal month for him. *Knowing that, and understanding it are two very different things*, she thought. There was no question she was worried that Patrick might be having second thoughts about their relationship. And, she knew better than to let her imagination play ping-pong with her emotions, but she couldn't help it. She was trying so hard not to think about how she might have given him the wrong signals, but it wasn't working.

During her weakest moments, when her negative thoughts ran amok, all the restless notions made her feel disconnected from him; made her feel unsure and off balance, and she'd question herself: *Maybe it's because I'm a single mom? Maybe it's because I'm a country bumpkin and he's a big-city lawyer?*

Here she was, with this beautiful child growing faster than green beans in a summer garden, a beautiful, loving, and thoughtful man wanting her, and still, she found herself fighting the specters from her past. Her mind drifted. Comforting memories pushed through her negative thoughts, and she saw herself as a little girl, standing at the kitchen table laughing and watching her father kiss her mother as they made breakfast together during a bright and sunny spring morning.

She could almost smell the newly turned earth as a gentle breeze brought it into the farmhouse. She closed her eyes to try and catch the rich, earthy scent of it. Then, as if from above, she saw herself sitting on her father's lap, driving the tractor, and plowing the field for next year's planting.

How she loved those memories. More precious than jewels to her. But the girl she had been back then was far behind her now, lost in some distant valley of bad dreams and nightmares never to return, and the woman she was becoming was ready for happier and more pleasant dreams.

She thought of Patrick and the love and support he offered her, and her spirit floated back to her. The truth of the matter was, the time she spent with Patrick had become a valuable treasure. Something not to be squandered. To do so would be reckless and foolish. His compassion and understanding had rejuvenated the simple pleasures of being with a man—pleasures she thought would never reach the surface again.

If Patrick left her, she'd be lost again. Drowning, again.

The entire time Patrick had been away, she hadn't cried one time.

It came out now, all at once.

❧ ❖ ❦

Winter held Chelsea in her arms, kissed her, wetting Chelsea's cheek with the last of her tears. They gazed out the living room window and watched a gentle fall of the first winter snowflakes filling the late October sky like millions of miniature doves—first snow of the year. Winter's mind reached back once again to a memory of her mother telling her, when she was a child, that whatever day you saw the first snowflake floating down from the sky, that day would tell you how many days it would snow all winter long.

She held Chelsea closer, kissed her on the cheek once again as they watched more snowflakes silently fall and cover the ground, quilting it in white. It took a few more tissues to sop up the leftover renegade tears. Having a good cry, watching the snow, and of course, having Chelsea snuggled tightly to her bosom, helped Winter find peace of mind.

In truth, after the big cry, she felt better than she had in days. So, instead of dwelling on her past, she was going to embrace the excitement, the uncertainty, the mystery of the journey she and Patrick were sharing. *"Out with the old and in with the new."* It may be an old saying, but it's a good one, she thought. It reminded her how every year at the stroke of midnight on New Year's Eve, it was the one and only time she could kiss the old year goodbye and kiss the new year hello. That's what she wanted to do with Patrick, wave goodbye to her past and say hello to her future. She took in a long breath, let it out, and let her anxiety go with it.

The vacuum that lived inside her each day had been replaced with the longing to love Patrick completely, unconditionally, without fear. When she and Patrick were together, she felt fearless, as if they could do anything together. She'd be damned if she'd let the misfortunes of her past displace her happiness with Patrick, who was so willing to love her and her daughter, without judging, despite her faults and insecurities.

She was surprised with her inner vehemence, but finally, after so many years of sadness, she was ready to work beyond the adversity she'd stumbled over. She had a choice to make. She could choose a life where compassion, laughter, and love could exist alongside the lightning strikes that might happen and accept whatever came her way or live a life where sorrow made the rules. To say it in a flowery way: *Winter could either remain a slave to her past, or let love heal the torn edges of her heart.*

❧ ◆ ❧

Winter missed Patrick. No doubt about it. She missed everything about him. She missed the sparkle in his baby blues when he'd tease her, and the way they crinkled at the corners when he smiled. She missed how she felt when he held her in his arms, safe and secure . . . how his fingers sank into her hair, holding her to him as if he couldn't get close enough to her . . . or how when he touched her, her entire body would shiver.

She loved him for his strength of character, his sense of humor, the depth of caring for his friends. Patrick was like a soothing balm. No way could she have stopped the inevitable, nor would she have wanted to. She let the words tumble out echoing all around her like a warm, cozy pair of sweatpants.

I love him, I love him . . . I love him!

⁂

A sudden knock at the door interrupted Winter's thoughts.

A large package. Winter signed for it and carried it into the living room and was surprised to find her heart pounding and her face warming. She couldn't hold her fingers still to open the box. Chelsea opened it, and inside the large package were four more boxes.

She and Chelsea lined each box in a row on the floor, from the largest to the smallest. For a short and quiet moment, she gazed at the boxes. The image of Patrick kissing her jumped into her thoughts and made her flush. Before she could take her next breath, Chelsea had taken the top off the biggest box and pushed aside the white tissue paper.

"It's beautiful, mom." In the big box was a black evening gown with a simple but elegant taffeta floor-length skirt.

"It is beautiful," Winter said, more to herself than to Chelsea, and held the dress under her chin and pressed it next to her body. The gown had a wraparound bodice cut high on the waist and sprinkled with tiny seed pearls. Its deceptively simple tailoring combined with the soft luxuriousness of the fabric made it feel and look custom-made especially for her.

When she tried it on, it felt weightless and was fluid when she moved. It was sensual. It was perfect. The other boxes offered a matching black embroidered shawl with elbow-length black gloves, an elegant pearl necklace, and a pair of black peau de soie shoes.

Back At the Lodge With Winter

Winter stopped talking and glanced at me as if only realizing for the first time that we had been sitting in the back-yard of the lodge for half the night, enjoying a cozy fire and good conversation. She said to me, "When I tried the shoes on, they were light as air. Perfect for dancin'." Then she was quiet, drifting back to the memory with a warm, contented look softening her face. I didn't break the silence. Winter's full lips pulled into a wide smile, and I lowered my brow, begging her to tell me more. "A—n-n-d . . . ," I said, drawing the word out as long as I could. I could see the sheen in her eyes.

She copied me, "W—e-l-l-l . . . you're gonna think I'm silly. They may not have been glass slippers but they sure felt good on my feet."

I laughed, touched her arm and gave her a gentle squeeze and said, "I really like this guy." She smiled and told me when she put the dress and shoes on, she and Chelsea danced around their tiny living room, in their small rented home, with the snow falling outside, laughing and singing, and feeling like princesses.

"I really thought I'd lost him," she said, and once again her eyes sparkled.

She told me that she still wasn't sure whether she could be bold enough to go to the ball, but receiving such a unique and thoughtful gift was more than sufficient to melt any woman's heart and keep her head turned in the right direction.

৻৲

After Winter received the gifts from Patrick, all the insecurities that tried to crush her faded away. She felt silly for agonizing over such emotions but thought that it was a woman's right to do so.

"Patrick wrote a note," she said.

"Great. Just what you need—another note," I replied.

"You'll like this one," she said with a broad smile.

Winter pulled the note out of her purse and gave it to me to read.

I read it out loud:

My Beautiful Winter,

I didn't know your size, but if you need to exchange any-thing, go to the store. They know you might be coming.

Enclosed are directions to the ball. Please come and stand by my side so I can stand by yours. I want the chance to whisper in your ear I love you.

You don't know how many times I wake up in the middle of the night and wish you were lying next to me, and how I want you to take my hand so I could give you all of me for the rest of my days.

The thing is, Winter, you are my chance for happiness.

When we're together, you make me feel like the impossible is possible. There is nothing I possess, or ever will possess, that could ever be as priceless as you. If you come to the ball, you can look into my eyes and know exactly how I feel, and see I have no doubts.

Please come!

From my heart to yours, always,

— Pat

"Nice note," I said. I reread the note before I handed it back to her and placidly said, "Really—it's a nice note. I believe him."

In a voice that was soft with no regret, she spoke to the fire, her eyebrows drawing together. "I believe him, too—I don't know . . ."

"Hold on . . ." I cut her off before she could say anything else. "I wanna hear the rest," I said. "—but I need more coffee. Don't go anywhere." I got up, pointed my finger at her and added, "I mean it, stay put." I took our coffee cups and walked back into the lodge for refills. When I returned, I handed her cup back to her and sat down. The steam from the coffee brushed across her face like little, wispy, dancing spirits, and evaporated before she'd finished her first sip. Her eyes were glued to the fire, and as I watched, they squinted, as if an idea had found its way out of the fog. I could tell she was still emotionally caught but looking past everything as if suddenly seeing things in a different perspective.

But I think what was really going on was the hope of a chapel resting on her heart—a looming hope dangling at the edge of a cliff, that, perhaps she had actually found someone exceptional. So I continued to sit with her and let the hiss and sizzle from the fire be the only sounds interrupting the silence that connected us.

Winter was not looking at me, and it was evident, based on my observation, she was more pensive than merely quiet. Then I noticed she was still holding the note in her hand, examining it purposely, as if reading it for the very first time. When she realized I'd been watching her, she carefully refolded it as if it were an ancient and irreplaceable manuscript, and placed it back in her purse.

She took another sip of coffee, and said, "Hold this," extending her cup to me, then added, "—an' this." Handing me her hat. She wrapped the back of her hair into a loose knot and struck it through with two long pins from her purse. I have to admit, the smooth motion of a lady's hands as they shape their hair is a purely feminine trait, which I adore. It's an unconscious movement so natural for a woman, and yet so remarkably appealing to me that it makes me pause.

I shook myself out of my gaze and teased, trying to cheer her up, "Hey? I think them-thar chapel bells are a-ringin'." And then I added, "If that note isn't a proposal, then I don't know what is—and, you have it in writing—from an attorney."

She dropped her head to her palms and dug the heels of her hands with her eyes. Her cheeks flushed, and I barely had time to say another word before she said, "Jeez Thomas, I've always jumped in too quickly."

"What's wrong with that?" I replied, as she reached over and took her hat and her coffee cup out of my hands. And then I said, "I say jump. Just because one guy in your life was a nut-job and another a loser, doesn't mean Patrick is going to be that way."

Her spine stiffened instantly, and she gave me a weak smile. "I'm so tired—I feel like I'm suspended between two worlds—" She was quiet for a moment, considered and then added, "— like a world that once was an' the other that might be."

She was quiet again, looking straight at me, challenging me, maybe hoping I'd have something witty and profound to add to the already witty and profound statement she had spouted.

At first, I was going to toss back some high-and-mighty spiritual Dalai Lama stuff, like, *"Trust the workings of the universe, (pause) . . . Nothing in this world happens, without reason, (long pause) . . . We are all firmly planted, exactly where we are supposed to be, (longer pause) . . . You were meant to experience great pain, (short pause) . . . to become the person you are today."* You know, the kind of wisdom that always has a lot of pauses in it for that dramatic flair. But I didn't. I couldn't—partly because I always waffle back and forth about Providence and partly because it seemed like such a trite thing to say. Plus, I was sure she had already figured out what she was going to do.

Then I thought I should tell her this: *To turn your back on this opportunity, when you have suffered such great loss, well, that would be a greater tragedy than all the others you've endured.*

The thought skirted the edge of my tongue less than a second. But I was exhausted from grasping for revelation to emphasize the remarkable qualities she and Patrick had to give each other.

The words were too heavy to release.

I couldn't say it.

Instead, I broke the silence and threw the obvious question back at her, "Well . . . Halloween is tomorrow night, and?" I tilted my head to one side and gazed straight back at her, leaning in closer to her, trying my best impersonation of puppy-dog eyes. She didn't respond—just smiled, and I felt like a Twinkie again. I should have gone the other way and voiced my *"great loss and suffering"* homily.

It was getting late, and I suddenly realized just how late it was. Almost midnight. And getting colder, too. When I spoke, my breath made visible wisps. "You *are* going to the ball, right?" I asked.

She still didn't reply, as if making up her mind, or just being Winter and trying to keep me in suspense.

"Are you going or not?" I asked again, shifting in my chair, actually getting impatient with her. She vacantly stared into the fire. I could tell she was dreaming about being with Patrick at the ball.

Then she said, more to herself, than to me, "Am I going to the ball—well . . ." Her lips lifted in a hint of a playful smile, deepening her dimple, and added, "That *is* the question, isn't it?" I could see it in her eyes, a slight shift, or twitch. The thought seemed to strike her, but not uncomfortably so. "I'm different now," she said as she straightened herself in the chair. She pulled her scarf apart, redoing it, but tied it differently this time, then tossed her coffee cup into the flames. The fire blazed for a brief moment. She turned back to face me and studied me with a deliberate but caring effort, with her alluring green and weathered eyes. I'll never forget those eyes.

I shivered. But only a little.

The short-lived radiance from the flaming cup settled, and the amber firelight highlighted and danced with shadows, playing with the soft, delicate features of her face, giving her cheeks a seductive glow.

Patrick was lucky to have her, I thought. And she, him.

She gave me the most provocative and unforgettable wide smile like a big, fat, sly, and hungry cat looking at a plump canary. And her voice had that kittenish quality when she said, "It's gettin' late." Then she smiled with a little giggle and teased me, "I might turn into a pumpkin."

She stood to leave, put her hand on my shoulder, and rubbed it with a thoughtful touch. I stood up, too, and she surprised me by giving me a friendly hug. When I felt her body touch mine, I wanted to hold onto her and not let go, but she gently pushed away from me, leaving the smallest gap between us, and gave me a polite smile and kissed me softly on my cheek—which I felt move all the way through me.

"You're not going to tell me, are you?" I asked.

She moved to my ear as if she was going to kiss me again, and I was eager that she would, but instead, she whispered, "Thanks for being my friend." And when she looked directly into my eyes, I felt a jolt one gets from being pierced by a stare that's known disappointment, faced it, and won.

"Friends forever," I said. She looked away. For a moment, her face expressed a reaction I couldn't quite grasp. When she turned her head back to me, her eyes appeared pensive. And when she spoke her voice was kind, affectionate.

"You're a good man, Thomas." Then she sashayed off, not saying another word, waving an arm goodbye, not looking back. Right then and there, at that very moment, Winter was walking out of my life, and I knew I had to let her go.

I sat back down, and for some time after Winter left, I watched and waited for the fire to die down. It didn't take long for it to mellow until all that was left was nothing but the soft red glow of embers and an occasional crackle.

I threw my coffee cup onto the glowing mound and watched it blaze with a fiery passion, edges erupting into a bright orange, then turning to ash. I followed the ash as some drifted up, pushed away by the heat of the fire until it broke apart spreading out with the breeze. I always get a strange sensation after someone tells me his or her story. It's a rich and thought-ful aftertaste that sticks to my mind for the longest time, until I decompress and write it down and release it.

While I stared at the crepitating glow, my mind relived all of what she confided in me. I came up with something I wished I had told her the second she gave me that hug. I wished I had said, "*You have a chance to have your happiness. I only hope you have the heart to take that chance.*" (I think her kiss threw me off.)

Funny, isn't it, how we always seem to find the right thing

to say to someone after they're gone? Then again, maybe my telling her to jump in was exactly what she needed to hear?

I don't know. I do hope so.

I guess I desperately wanted her to push fear aside and take the leap. But fear of the unknown for many people is a potent trigger that, more often than not, will hold a person back from taking that cavernous dive into love.

Sometimes, when love rolls upon us, it's better not to think so much. Sometimes we have to push worry and fear out of the way and let things fall where they may because magic moments can vanish in the blink of an eye.

But fear and grief are sly and crafty beasts working in tandem. Perhaps one is never over it.

Maybe when lightning strikes enough times in a person's life, they will always stay inside their protective shell when there's a thunderstorm.

I simply do not know.

I do believe once we open our hearts to the magic of things, things happen: something we might be feeling one moment—self-pity, or sorrow, perhaps—can vanish, like the snap of a finger, gone in an instant. Everything we had been grappling with is shaken right out of us leaving us free to feel what we hadn't felt, or thought we might not ever feel again—hope, love, passion—all the significant little bits that make us embrace life and its unbridled mysteries. The problem is, as we grow older, the wraiths from our past become harder to keep hidden while we seek to find contentment in our lives. The dolefulness we think we can suppress, those horrible lightning strikes that can drop us to our knees, the pain we hope no one will ever discover, are harder to camouflage over time no matter how much we long earnestly for tranquility.

It was my hope that Winter's fears would grow smaller, become less important once she realized that none of us are able to entirely escape our past, that life will always twist and turn in the most unexpected ways, and it's okay to end up in a different place than where we thought we would find happiness.

I learned a long time ago: people can run, hide, and ignore the tragedies of their lives for only so long. No matter what, at some point, grief will find its way back and force us to deal with the pain. The thing about grief is, it will do one of two things, It will hold you down in that sickly sentiment, make you weak, and consume you, or it will make you stronger. Knowing Winter, even for such a short time as I did, I knew it would make her stronger.

৵

Was I envious of Patrick? Of course.

Was I happy for Winter? Absolutely.

Do I have any regrets about Winter? Some.

But I don't regret for an instant that Winter and I had the type of relationship we had. It wasn't the bond that makes a couple run off together for a weekend tryst in the Catskills or zip up and snuggle in a side-by-side sleeping bag. Or take the marriage plunge.

We had a good friendship. Firm and true.

And opening her heart to me as a friend, as I did for her,

we conferred a value on it. It is a currency we will never spend. A gift I will forever keep in my wallet and take out whenever my spirit needs lifting.

And I loved her for that.

∾

The next day, when I went back to work, Winter wasn't there. I found out she had the weekend off, which gave me hope that she might have actually gone to the ball.

She didn't show up for work the following week either, and no one at the lodge had any idea what happened to her. A few weeks later, I asked my boss about Winter and was told she wasn't working at the lodge anymore.

I never saw her again after the night she told me her story. And it seemed I was the only one at the lodge who had any inkling as to what might have happened to her.

One of my coworkers said a friend of a friend thought they saw her slinging hash at Forkey's, a family restaurant in Martinsville, which is not that far from Bloomington.

Another heard she went back to her loser of a boyfriend, Frankie, and had another baby. Another said she had heard that Winter married some fancy-schmancy, rich lawyer down in Kentucky somewhere, and she was breeding horses on her own farm, and her daughter Chelsea had won her first barrel racing competition at the Kentucky State Fair.

That rumor was my favorite because I started it. It was my wish, my dream for Winter to have that kind of happy ending. And as each month worked into the next, a new and revised rumor would mosey through the corridors of the lodge and sit alongside the others. That's small-town gossip for you, which runs hot and heavy at the Abe Martin Lodge, and each decorative detail that crossed my path about Winter gave me an enjoyable chuckle, especially the one I started. Even now, as I finish telling you about Winter, I have no idea if she went to the ball or not.

In a way, I don't want to know. I like the mystery of it.

I love the daydream that I created in my mind of Winter standing on the first rung of a fence (wearing a baseball cap and cowgirl boots), looking out over a wide-open lush, green meadow with a sliced apple in the palm of her hand and feeding a roan horse of a whitish coat thickly speckled with black and gray. I like that image. It's where she belonged. It was in her blood, thick and heavy, yet graceful and fluent. It is my hope that Winter did find a small measure of peace, something we all seek but few of us ever find. And when she walked away from me that October evening, open and available, I liked that smile she gave me. Maybe, too, I wanted to keep the memory of her sneaky fat-cat-like grin all to myself. It was a good smile. Yes, and the kiss, too.

I'll never forget her kiss. Every time I think of that sweet, gentle kiss she planted on my cheek, my face heats up, and I get the most delightful tingle. That night will always be a lovely memory I can replay each time Winter finds her way into my dreams.

                    ❦

Between you and me . . . well . . . I imagine Winter walking into the ballroom at the Halloween dance wearing that stunning black evening gown with seed pearls on the bodice. I can see it bright and crisp, as a cloud-splattered, breezy blue day.

She looks beautiful.

Red hair glowing, cheeks to match.

She's standing alone at the top of the stairs of a large, open, alabaster staircase, and her pearl necklace is sparkling in the crystal chandelier light.

You might think me silly comparing Winter to Cinderella.

But I can't help myself.

As I mentioned at the beginning of this tale, I am a push-over when it comes to things of the heart.

There is a part of me that really likes that kind of stuff.

I believe in miracles.

I believe good things should happen to good people.

I believe that life isn't made up of only two colors, black-and-white but moves through a multitude of shades, more color than a box of Crayolas.

I can smell it. Taste it. Waxy and sharp.

That is how I usually see things. See life. Through an unlimited variety and intonations of color.

Rich. Vibrant. Unexpected. Swirling and smashed into my footsteps.

And knowing me the way you do now, I know you know what happens next:

It's the same happily-ever-after tale,
about a princess and a prince, that has been told and retold
in story and in song a thousand times over
and will continue to be told again,

and again,
for a thousand times more.

Winter's ravishing princess-like gown is flowing effortlessly, pushing gently against her body as she walks down the stairs.

At the bottom of the stairs, of course, would be Patrick.

Winter would hesitate only briefly, smile and then carefully descend. Patrick would joyfully bound up the stairs, and they would meet halfway. He'd reach for Winter with an outstretched hand. She'd accept, placing her hand in his. There would be a moment of dreamy, star-struck staring into each other's eyes with bright anticipation.

The ball, I am sure, would look like all grand galas, with women sparkling all over the dance floor like daisies prancing among penguins. And there, in the middle of it all, would be Winter, waltzing with her Patrick—she, the only rose at the ball.

Now wouldn't that be something . . .

It is our duty, nay,
it is our responsibility to ask questions and wonder,
So we can understand where we came from
and where we are going,
So we don't make the same mistakes
over and over . . .

Excerpts from the author's journal, Skaters Rule.

— Oahu, Hawaii, Monday, February 09, 1998

Never thought I'd be coaching figure skating in Hawaii.
It's been a unique experience, and I've met some terrific people.
I've become good friends with many of the skating families. They
have opened their hearts and their homes to me. Friendships that
will last a lifetime. No doubt about it.
One family asked me to be a godfather to their new baby daughter.
I was so taken aback and humbled, I accepted immediately.
However, when asked to change a diaper, I yielded to the mere
thought of what kind of surprise I might find within.
Not really sure how much longer I'm going to stay around here and
coach, though.
Beginning to feel the need to see a stretch of blacktop that disappears
into the horizon, instead of going 'round in circles.

*   *   *

— Sunday, April 15, 2001

Dillingham Airfield, North Shore, Oahu, Hawaii

There are patches of the night sky on Oahu where the stars gather
for a galactic gala like nothing I have ever seen.
They foxtrot across the black with so much grace it brings
involuntary tears to my eyes.
At times, the jamboree is so dazzling their luster glows as
bright as a full moon, casting a brilliant shine upon the truth.
Magical.
Perfect.
But the sad thing is, this is not where I belong.
Time for me to move on.
Time for me to go home.

Epilogue

Chasing Happiness

Early Evening: Years later.
First day of spring.
Daffodils are blooming!
When it's my time to depart this earthly realm,
I'm going to miss everything so much!
Do I have regrets? Absolutely.
Given a chance to go back in time and make changes,
I would. I would have tried harder to convince my dear
Martha, my high school sweetheart, to travel with me,
and I would never have worn bell-bottom pants.

Both my parents became ill a few years ago. I returned to my hometown, bought a house, and made a home for them so I could care for their needs during their last days—family first, above all else. It was difficult for me to see them so susceptible to the ravages of old age, the loss of dignity, and the deliberate betrayal of their bodies by forces no one can master.

It changed me.

They both have passed, and today, Winter raided my thoughts about the tragedies she faced and the courage it took for her to fight the demons that tried to clamp down on her.

It inspired me to put pencil to paper once again.

❧

Thinking of Winter, and all she coped with, made me more aware of the monster I will be facing soon. I only hope I will be able to find a fraction of her courage to exchange blows with the beast of which I am about to challenge.

It's been years since that chilly October evening when Winter and I had our chat by the fire. And to this very day, whispering in the back of my mind is the mist of her soul that has imprinted itself on my heart. I cherish the time we spent together. I would have loved the chance of falling into a Winter of my own and having her fall back into me.

One image that rises above the clouds more than others was the way she did her hair the night she told me her story. I can see her tying it around in a loose knot as if it happened yesterday, and I catch myself smiling. Each time that smile stretches across my face, I let out a soft breath with a soft sigh, and it fills me, prickles my skin, and brings color to my cheeks.

It wasn't long after Winter walked out of my life that I remembered such a moment as I just described when Winter sauntered back into my mind. I was still working at the lodge, and my good-ole set-up buddy Simon and I had been rolling big, round, six-foot wooden tables into the reception hall for a wedding—twenty-two in all. Believe you me, rolling and balancing those big round tables is an art in and of itself. For no apparent reason, Winter flashed into my mind, and I was grinning like a ghost on Halloween.

Simon yelled at me, "Whatcha grinnin' at, bub?"

My mind wavered as if in a draft, affected by the image of Winter, and my temporary inability to recognize my surroundings. I realized I had been standing absolutely still in the middle of the room, holding the wooden table upright, staring vacantly into the past, caught in the haze of my thoughts. "Nothing, just grinnin'!" I yelled back.

It was a couple of months later I put in my two weeks notice. On my last day, I gave Simon ten Bic lighters and two cartons of Marlboro cigarettes. I thought it would keep him flush for a while, and in a way, I guess I was helping Natty, too.

You know what Simon said to me when I gave him the cigarettes? He said, "Thanks for the smokes, bub—alright if I give Natty some?" He looked at me with sincere eyes actually asking my permission, and added, "She's runnin' low."

I replied, "I think that'd be a great idea."

And that was the end of my days working at the Abe Martin Lodge.

✖

A man in his eighties named Shelby Perkins (everyone called him Shell), who I met in Muscatine, Iowa, said to me once, *If you live an ordinary life, then you'll have ordinary stories.* Then he went on to say, *But if you live a life full of adventure, you'll have extraordinary stories.* I think Shell was partially right, but I find his comment somewhat limiting. A person's story doesn't have to be full of adventure or have lightning strikes or miracles to make it special. It can be a sweet, simple story about two children trying to catch a rabbit with a carrot on a perfect spring morning, using a string and a soapbox crate, giggling and eating peanut butter and jelly sandwiches. Or, it can be a story like Winter's story, about a deserving woman chasing after, and trying to hold onto happiness. An average woman, wanting a normal life, to love and be loved. In my opinion, that life would be filled with beautiful and unexpected adventures, extraordinary in its own right.

↫

In all my travels, in all the small towns I've lived in, all the people I have ever met who had a story to tell, all had one thread in common, the chase for happiness.

I have always chased that which excites me. And what excites me is what gives value to my life, makes me feel worthwhile, and plops passion into my soul like Alka-Seltzer into water. For me, the most prominent strand that keeps me tied together, grounding me, and has brought excitement and pleasure to my life, has been my writing. It is then, when I am writing my stories that I am the happiest—the most at peace with myself.

I've been a witness to so many stories, so many lives lived in so many different ways, a rosary of memories anchored to my spirit, and I feel blessed that all those I have met have been willing to tell me their tales.

↫

When I started writing this manuscript about Winter's life,

I had turned forty-two only a few days before, and throughout the years I've rewritten chapters and added new ones. I thought, back then, I still had plenty of time to find my happily-ever-after. But fate found many ways of tying my shoelaces together, reshaping my path and altering my direction. The dreams I had in my youth—the hunger for drifting that seemed to fill all my needs then, the excitement of hearing people's stories—are far less important to me now.

At this time in my life, my mind is obsessively gripped by my mortality. I wonder what will happen with my immortal soul—if you believe in that sort of thing—and question my deeds here on earth, which would significantly affect whether I'll be sent down the long slide to fire and brimstone rather than the heavenly climb to angels.

With this on my conscious mind, my musing always gravitates to one thought that is forever suspended at the edge of my reasoning, *I have so many stories I want to tell, but not enough time to tell them all.*

❧

It is evident to me now that Winter and Patrick were like two pieces of cosmic dust traveling through the vast distances of the universe, dodging comets and meteors, moving in a timeless dance through the events that unfolded in their lives. And each and every celestial body they encountered purposefully pushed and pulled them, this way and that, nudging them closer to each other, inch by inch, guiding them to a single point in time.

Even though they had both been unaware of each other,

there was an unstoppable force quietly singing in the background of their lives that made sure, one day, they would meet.

We should all be so fortunate.

❧

And that, my dear friend, is Winter's story. One story among thousands that travel the roads over Brown County.

With each and every story
we write with our lives,
there will be only
one ending . . .

Excerpt from the author's journal, On The Road.

— Sunday, Mother's Day, May 13, 2001
My Birthday

Returned home to take care of my parents.
If there is one thing I have ever done right in my life,
it would be this.
They gave me more than love.
They gave me life.
Now I will repay them and be by their side to the very end.

AFTERTHOUGHTS

Author's Note

I was born with the name, Thomas Simms and raised in a small farming and industrial community, Columbus, Indiana. Columbus is about forty-five miles south of Indianapolis, sandwiched between fields of corn and soybeans, rolling hills of hardwood forests, and Cummins diesel engines.

This story, meeting Winter, my travels across the country, coaching figure skating, doing pantomime in elementary schools, the odd jobs, everything, it's all true. What I enjoyed the most, was drifting from town to town across the United States, eating in home-style family roadside, or downtown restaurants, with long counters and booths, and getting to know people like Winter.

I fell in love with writing and illustrating, especially children's picture books when I was in junior high school. That's when I received my first rejection letter from a publisher. By the time I was in my twenties, I had accumulated enough rejection letters to fill three binders. It was then I decided maybe William

299

Shakespeare was right when he wrote, "What's in a name?" So I changed my name and now use my great-great-grandfather's name, T. C. Bartlett.

Other than that, *Roads Over Brown County* remains as it is, a tribute to a woman who never gave up her pursuit of happiness. As should we all. —T. C. Bartlett

Photo by David Leonardi · Lake Placid Summer Ice Dance Competition 1972

Excerpt from the author's journal, Skaters Rule.

— Friday, June 26, 1970
Squaw Valley Figure Skating Camp

I am holding a bag of ice on my left eye. The chill of it makes me laugh, but when I laugh, I can feel the sting of the punch. My skating buddy and partner in crime, Charlie, is holding a bag of ice on his right cheek, which is reddish orange like a ripe Georgia peach. The three dudes from the basketball camp are nursing ice bags, too, and looking as ragged as we are.

There is more than one athletic training camp here in Squaw besides figure skating. There's a basketball camp and our favorite, the cheerleading camp. Oh my, you should see all the girls . . . I'll write more about that later, as I have a date with one of the cheerleaders tonight . . .

But for the past couple of days when Charlie and I were at the rink practicing, the three basketball dudes sat up in the stands and called us pansies and fags, and clapped when we'd fall.

At first, we decided to let it go and just skate. Today, however, we didn't. When the heckling began, we yanked off our skates, vaulted onto the barrier, shinnied up and over the balcony into the stands . . . it was a good fight, fists flying everywhere . . . three ballplayers against two pansy (ha) figure skaters . . . nobody won.

Our coach, however, Jimmy Grogan, and the basketball coach didn't agree with our tactics. They're making the basketball players put on rental skates and practice with us, and then the five of us have to hit the courts. A game to one hundred.

That should be interesting . . . so far, skaters rule!

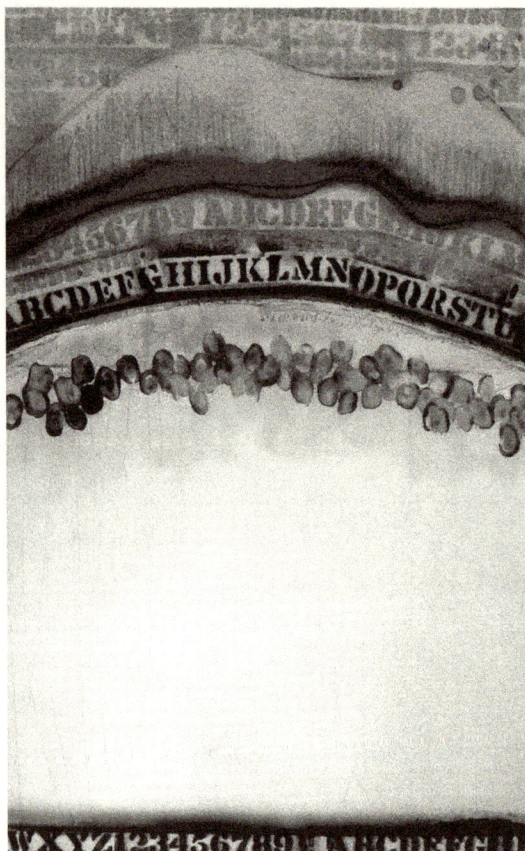

Papaver Alphabet, 1987.
Acrylic, Ink & Plexiglas On Canvas, 3.5 x 2.5 ft.

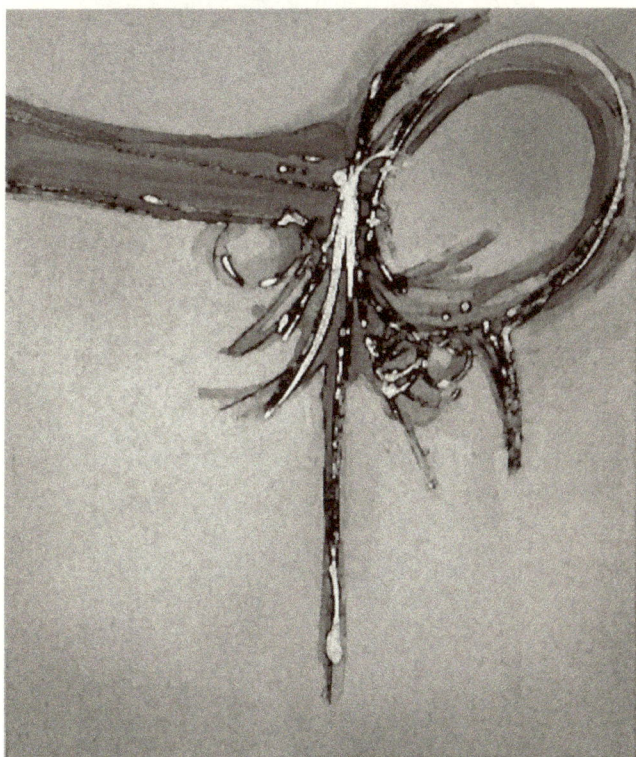

Dancer, 1978.
Acrylic, Graphite, & Ink On Canvas, 6 x 4 ft.

Prairie, 1978. Acrylic, Graphite, String &
Rice Paper On Canvas, 2.5 x 1.5 ft.

ABOUT THE TYPE

The font styles for this book are:

Goudy Old Style
Herculanum
Thomas's Hand - Designed by T. C. Bartlett
Monotype Corsiva

SANDHILL PUBLISHERS, LLC

AN AMERICAN PUBLISHING COMPANY